TALENT, WONDER & DELIGHT

A Scrapbook of Victorian Entertainment

TIPTON WAKE!

Important Notice—Stop and Read!

GREAT BACCHANALIAN

DEMONSTRATION!

WILL BE HELD

AT TIPTON WAKE,

JULY, 1869.

His Royal Highness King Alcohol,

Has great pleasure in informing his numerous subjects, that he will endeavour to render this Wake most interesting, amusing, and enchanting for all classes of subjects in his dominions, that he has engaged the active services of his long tried and successful Officers, Flaming Gin, Sparkling Wine, Muddy Porter, and Frothy Ale, who will all of them be in active attendance. Each day's diversion to commence with Music, Dancing, Singing, and Drinking, to be carried on with Gambling, Nine-pins, &c., in which His Majesty hopes all his loyal subjects will heartily engage; the same to close in the usual way, with Drunkenness, Swearing, Fighting, Brawling, Reeling, and Wife Beating, Empty Pockets, Aching Heads, Black Eyes, perhaps Broken Bones, Fractured Skulls, and Loss of Life: Hard Hearts, Seared Consciences, Benumbed Affections, Depraved Minds, Polluted Morals, Loss of Property, Time, and Health, Premature Graves, Weeping Widows, Orphan Children, Crowded Unions, Full Gaols, with every other Physical, Mental, and Moral Evil connecting itself with this World. Prospects Gloomy, and Souls ruined to all Eternity.

N.B.—King Alcohol has, in order to render the whole as effective as possible, engaged the services of HIS SATANIC MAJESTY, THE DEVIL, who will preside over the whole affair.

A temperance poster
(reproduced from Folklore and Songs of the Black Country)

TALENT, WONDER & DELIGHT

A Scrapbook of Victorian Entertainment

Anthony Adams & Robert Leach

BLACKIE

Blackie & Son Limited
Bishopbriggs, Glasgow G64 2NZ
450/452 Edgware Road, London W2 1EG

© Anthony Adams and Robert Leach 1976
First published 1976

Educational Edition ISBN 0 216 90052 2
General Edition ISBN 0 216 90051 4

Printed in Great Britain by
Robert MacLehose & Company Limited, Glasgow

Foreword

Talent, wonder and delight sums up an important aspect of the Victorian Age. It was an age in which there was always something new to be seen and wondered at.

In preparing this book we found that the conventional view of the Victorians as sober-suited, decorous and high-minded individuals, dedicated to plain living, high thinking and unceasing manufactory, was confounded at every turn. We aim to give a taste of the bubbling mass of life underneath the severe Victorian surface.

Victoria's reign was a long one—from 1837 to 1901. We could not hope to cover every entertainment or all the vogues of the period, but we have tried to indicate the range of the Victorians' leisure-time activities. The early days of Victoria's reign have a flavour which is almost Regency—they are the days of the Song-and-Supper Rooms, Dorkin's Night on the stage, prize-fighting and badger-baiting. Later in the period, Henry Irving and Dan Leno set a more sophisticated tone on the stage, and football and cricket come into their own as sports. This gradual change of style may tell us something of where our first uninformed notions of Victorianism came from, though these later entertainers were hardly as staid as we sometimes imagine our great grandfathers to have been.

The two most notable writers on entertainment in the Victorian era were Charles Dickens and Henry Mayhew. But because their works are so well known we have deliberately omitted them from this collection in favour of less accessible pieces. However, a proper understanding of Victorian entertainment is impossible without taking account of Dickens and Mayhew, and we strongly recommend that their work is read in conjunction with what is here. Bound volumes of *Punch* for the period will also prove helpful in conveying something of the flavour of that extraordinary mixture of delights and wonders that made up the entertainment of the Victorian age.

ANTHONY ADAMS
ROBERT LEACH

Acknowledgments

For permission to reproduce copyright material in this anthology, the compilers and publishers would like to thank the following:

University Library, Cambridge for the photograph on page 2.
Mary Evans Picture Library for the photographs on pages 6, 28, 45, 56, 64, 72.
Cassell and Company Limited for the photograph on page 9 and for the extracts from *Cassell's Book of Indoor Amusements, Card Games and Fireside Fun*.
National Liberal Club for the photograph on page 13.
The Savoy Hotel for the facsimile on page 15.
Liverpool Public Library for the photograph on page 20.
Radio Times Hulton Picture Library for the photographs on pages 32, 60, 70, 87 (*top*).
The Raymond Mander and Joe Mitchenson Theatre Collection for the photograph on page 48.
Ascherberg, Hopwood & Crew Ltd for the song cover on page 35 and for the words and music of the song "Wotcher 'Ria".
Punch for the cartoon on page 58.
The Illustrated London News for the photograph on page 67.
Victoria and Albert Museum for the photograph on page 68.
Mr Tom Langley for the photograph on page 79.
Colorsport for the photograph on page 81.
Marylebone Cricket Club for the photograph on page 85.
John Frost Historical Newspaper Service for the photograph on page 87 (*foot*).

Oxford University Press for the extract from *Lark Rise to Candleford* by Flora Thompson.
Ginn & Co. Ltd for the words of "The Wedgefield Wake" from *Songs of a Changing World* edited by Jon Raven.
Peter Newbolt for the poem "Vitaï Lampada" by Sir Henry Newbolt.
H. Darewski Music Publishing Co., 138–40 Charing Cross Road, London WC2H 0LD for the words and music of the song "Come to Your Martha" by A. C. Vance.
The Administrators of the Estate of E. Gordon Craig for the extract from *Henry Irving* by E. G. Craig.

Every effort has been made to trace owners of copyright but in some cases this has not been possible. The publishers would, however, be glad to hear from any copyright owners not included.

Contents

Prologue

On the occasion of Queen Victoria's Coronation, festivities were held at Cambridge:

"Between 12 and 1 o'clock the Processions commenced. As the various parochial divisions converged to the place of their general meeting, the interest of the sight continued to increase. Streets choked up with people, all in their holiday clothes; thousands wending their way to one point; men, women, children—happy and merry; not an angry word to be heard; not the least pressure or confusion; not an attempt of any one to mend his position; not the slightest interference of policemen or constables, and no necessity for it! The parts of the town distant from Parker's Piece seemed to be in danger of being wholly depopulated. There appeared to be many whole streets without a single individual in them—we mean even in the houses. Hundreds of fathers had gone with their spouses, their sons and daughters, not forgetting their very infants, with plates, mugs, knives, and forks, to spend the remainder of the day on the Piece; and, as if it was not supposed that even a single person could be found to turn thief on such a day, the whole household property of the town seemed to be entirely trusted to the protection of Providence—and we will venture to say too, for the credit of our native town, with the most perfect security."

*　　*　　*　　*　　*

At 2 o'clock all the parties who were to partake of the banquet were assembled and seated, in number about 15,000: the number of spectators may be estimated at 17,000 more; making a total of 32,000 people assembled to witness and enjoy this grand festivity. The day was at this moment most splendid, the atmosphere clear, and the heat moderate.

*　　*　　*　　*　　*

Immediately the presidents, stewards, and carvers, at the several tables commenced their labours: joint after joint of the primest meat disappeared; bread and pickles were supplied in abundance; water in casks was provided for the *few* who chose to ask for it; and ale plentifully supplied to those who presented their tickets. To the meat

A VIEW of the GRAND FÊTE on PARKER'S PIECE, CAMBRIDGE, To celebrate the Coronation of HER MOST GRACIOUS MAJESTY QUEEN VICTORIA, June 28th 1838

Number of Persons seated to Dinner 15,000, supposed number of Spectators 17,000. TOTAL number persons 32,000.

succeeded such a supply of plum-puddings as never has been witnessed in this kingdom before. Admirable in quality, and smoking hot, they appeared on the tables and vanished again with a rapidity that might stand bail for their goodness. All around were thousands of smiling faces and of gladdened hearts; there was every possible comfort, no limitation of room, no jealousies, no bickerings; but harmony and satisfaction, which graced the occasion, and rendered pleasure doubly pleasing. It was a feast of happy multitudes, and yet a feast of *reason*, rarely combined with the utmost plenty: all disorder, intemperance, and selfishness seemed to have fled the spot, as if it were hallowed ground. And hallowed indeed it was, by cordial benevolence, by honest zeal, by firm loyalty, by heartfelt gratitude, by the praise of the pious heart lifted up to Him, who "filleth the hungry with good things".

During the demolition of the eatables, the Overture and Choral Finale were executed by a band of musical performers, and the choirs of Trinity and King's, with many members of the Choral Society, under the able and efficient conduct of Professor Walmisley.

In this interval also several small balloons were dispatched upon their aërial flight, and being wafted by the breeze over the tables, afforded much amusement, particularly one that caught fire at a good elevation, and was entirely consumed. These were succeeded, at the termination of the Anthem, by one of large dimensions, upwards of 18 feet high, formed in regal colours of purple and white, which was inflated upon Montgolfier's principle of rarefied air, and went off in grand style; its ascent was gradual and beautiful, and when at a certain altitude above the heads of the assembled crowd, it discharged a fire-work that exploded with a loud report; being thus relieved of a certain weight of ballast, it rapidly rose and attained a great elevation. This pretty specimen of aërostatic machinery formed an object of interest for half-an-hour, and was lost to sight in the distant horizon; though still making its way, it ultimately descended about five miles from the place of ascent, uninjured.

from *A Complete Account of the Proceedings Relating to the Festival Held at Cambridge in Honour of the Coronation of Her Most Gracious Majesty, Queen Victoria*

3

At Home

Leaving Cards

Leaving cards is the first step towards forming, or enlarging, a circle of acquaintances. A lady's visiting card should be printed in small, clear, copper-plate type, and free from any kind of embellishment. It should be a thin card, $3\frac{1}{2}$ inches in depth or even smaller. The name of the lady should be printed in the centre, and her address in the left-hand corner. It is now considered old-fashioned for husbands and wives to have their names printed on the same card: they should have separate cards of their own.

Leaving cards principally devolves upon the mistress of a house; a wife should leave cards for her husband as well as for herself. The master of a house has little or no card-leaving to do, beyond leaving cards upon his bachelor friends.

Mostly cards should be delivered in person, and not sent by post. A lady should desire her man-servant to inquire if the mistress of the house at which she is calling is "at home". If "not at home", she should hand him *three* cards: one of her own and two of her husband's; her card is left for the mistress of the house, and her husband's for both master and mistress. If the answer is in the affirmative, she should, after making the call, leave *two* of her husband's cards on the hall-table, and neither put them in the card-basket nor leave them on the drawing-room table, nor offer them to her hostess, all of which would be very incorrect.

When the mistress of the house has a grown-up daughter or daughters, the lady leaving cards should turn down one corner of her visiting card—the right-hand corner generally—to include the daughter or daughters in the call. Maiden ladies of a certain age should have visiting cards of their own.

from *Manners and Rules of Good Society*

4

Dinner Parties

DINNER BEING ANNOUNCED, the host offers his arm to, and places on his right hand at the dinner-table, the lady to whom he desires to pay most respect, either on account of her age, position, or from her being the greatest stranger in the party. If this lady be married and her husband present, the latter takes the hostess to her place at table, and seats himself at her right hand. The rest of the company follow in couples, as specified by the master and mistress of the house, arranging the party according to their rank and other circumstances which may be known to the host and hostess.

It will be found of great assistance to the placing of a party at the dinner-table, to have the names of the guests neatly (and correctly) written on small cards, and placed at that part of the table where it is desired they should sit. With respect to the number of guests, it has often been said, that a private dinner-party should consist of not less than the number of the Graces, or more than that of the Muses. A party of ten or twelve is, perhaps, in a general way, sufficient to enjoy themselves and be enjoyed. White kid gloves are worn by ladies at dinner-parties, but should be taken off before the business of dining commences.

*   *   *   *   *

WHEN DINNER IS FINISHED, THE DESSERT is placed on the table, accompanied with finger-glasses. It is the custom of some gentlemen to wet a corner of the napkin; but the hostess, whose behaviour will set the tone to all the ladies present, will merely wet the tips of her fingers, which will serve all the purposes required. The French and other continentals have a habit of gargling the mouth; but it is a custom which no English gentlewoman should, in the slightest degree, imitate.

WHEN FRUIT HAS BEEN TAKEN, and a glass or two of wine passed round, the time will have arrived when the hostess will rise, and thus give the signal for the ladies to leave the·gentlemen, and retire to the drawing-room. The gentlemen of the party will rise at the same time, and he who is nearest the door, will open it for the ladies, all remaining courteously standing until the last lady has withdrawn. Dr Johnson has a curious paragraph on the effects of a dinner on men. "Before dinner," he says, "men meet with great inequality of understanding; and those who are conscious of their inferiority have the modesty not to talk. When they have drunk wine, every man feels himself happy, and loses that modesty, and grows impudent and vociferous; but he is not improved, he is only not sensible of his defects." This is rather severe, but there may be truth in it.

In former times, when the bottle circulated freely amongst the guests, it was necessary for the ladies to retire earlier than they do at present, for the gentlemen of the company soon became unfit to conduct themselves with that decorum which is essential in the presence of ladies. Thanks, however, to the improvements in modern society, and the high example shown to the nation by its most illustrious personages, temperance is, in these happy days, a striking feature in the character of a gentleman. Delicacy of conduct towards the female sex has increased with the esteem in which they are now universally held, and thus, the very early withdrawing of the ladies from the dining-room is to be deprecated. A lull in the conversation will seasonably indicate the moment for the ladies' departure.

from *The Book of Household Management* by Mrs Isabella Beeton

A Victorian musical evening

A Very Busy Day

18th May 1837: This is a very buisy day as we are going to have a party this evening something larger than usual. We had four to dinner and about fifty or sixty in the evening. The plan of managing these parties are thus:— there were two men besides myself, one opened the door and let the Company in, I shewed them into a parlour where there was three maidservants to make tea and give it to them and take off their cloaks and bonnets, and the other man shewed them up into the drawingroom and gave in their names as lowd as he can bawl. There is very good singing and music in their way. After they have been here some time, we carrey them up some refreshments on trays and hand about amongst them. This is all kinds of sweet cakes and biscuits, lemonade, ashet, negos, orangade and many other pleasant drinks but the best is the different kind of ices. This is stuf made of ice pounded, mixed with cream, and juce of strawberry, some of apricot and oranges—in short, there are many different kinds. It's quite as cold as eating ice alone. It's eat out of glass sawsers with a spoon. It's from ten to sixteen shillings a quart, it depends on what fruit it's made of. The company comes jenerally about ten or eleven o'clock and stays until one or two in the morning. Sweet hearting matches are very often made up at these parties. It's quite disgusting to a modist eye to see the way the young ladies dress to atract the notice of the gentlemen. They are nearly naked to the waist, only just a little bit of dress hanging on the shoulder, the breasts are quite exposed except a little bit comeing up to hide the nipples. Plenty of false hair and teeth and paint. If a person wish to see the ways of the world, they must be a gentleman's servant, then they mite see it to perfection.

19th May 1837: Got up with a headache and feel stupid all day. Been out with the carriage this afternoon with Miss P. She kept me out longer than I thought she aught to have done, therefore I gave her a little row for it. I hope it will do her good. I served the old lady the same way the other day and it did her a deal of good, and I have no doubt that it will act the same in this case. Breakfast as usual, lunch seago and cold duck, dinner veal and minced mutton, soop and vegitables, pudding.

extract from the diary of William Taylor, footman, from *Useful Toil*

An Evening at Home

August 27.   Carrie and Mrs James went off shopping, and had not returned when I came back from the office. Judging from the subsequent conversation, I am afraid Mrs James is filling Carrie's head with a lot of nonsense about dress. I walked over to Gowing's and asked him to drop in to supper, and make things pleasant.

Carrie prepared a little extemporised supper, consisting of the remainder of the cold joint, a small piece of salmon (which I was to refuse, in case there was not enough to go round), and a blanc-mange and custards. There was also a decanter of port and some jam puffs on the sideboard. Mrs James made us play rather a good game of cards, called "Muggings". To my surprise, in fact disgust, Lupin got up in the middle, and, in a most sarcastic tone, said: "Pardon me, this sort of thing is too fast for me. I shall go and enjoy a quiet game of marbles in the back-garden."

Things might have become rather disagreeable but for Gowing (who seems to have taken to Lupin) suggesting they should invent games. Lupin said: "Let's play 'monkeys'. " He then led Gowing all round the room, and brought him in front of the looking-glass. I must confess I laughed heartily at this. I was a little vexed at everybody subsequently laughing at some joke which they did not explain, and it was only on going to bed I discovered I must have been walking about all the evening with an antimacassar on one button of my coat-tails.

from Diary of a Nobody by George and Weedon Grossmith

Indoor Amusements

A small flossy feather with very little stem must be procured. The players then draw their chairs in a circle as closely together as possible. One of the party begins the game by throwing the feather into the air as high as possible above the centre of the ring formed. The object of the game is to keep it from touching any one, as the player whom it touches must pay a forfeit; and it is impossible to imagine the excitement that can be produced by each player preventing the feather from alighting upon him. The game must be heartily played to be fully appreciated, not only by the real actors of the performance, but by the spectators of the scene. Indeed, so absurd generally is the picture presented, that it is difficult to say whether the players or the watchers have the most fun.

from *Cassell's Book of Indoor Amusements, Card Games and Fireside Fun*

Blind
Man's
Buff

Nine
Pins

Whist

Parlour
Magic

Fireside Fun

Forfeits

As an evening spent in playing round games would be thought incomplete if at the end of it the forfeits were not redeemed, so our book of amusements would be sadly lacking in interest if a list of forfeits were not provided. Indeed, many young people think that the forfeits are greater fun than the games themselves, and that the best part of the evening begins when forfeit time arrives. Still, although we will give a list of forfeits, it is by no means necessary that in the crying of them none but certain prescribed ones should be used. . . .

1. *Bite an inch off the poker.* This is done by holding the poker the distance of an inch from the mouth, and performing an imaginary bite.

2. *Kiss the lady you love best without anyone knowing it.* To do this the gentleman must of course kiss all the ladies present, the one he most admires taking her turn among the rest. . . .

5. *Put yourself through the keyhole.* To do this the word "Yourself" is written upon a piece of paper, which is rolled up and passed through the keyhole.

10. *Shake a sixpence off the forehead.* It is astonishing how even the most acute player may be deceived by this sixpenny imposition. The presiding genius, holding in his fingers a sixpence, proceeds with an air of great importance to fasten the coin upon the forehead of the victim, by means of first wetting it, and then pressing it firmly just above the eyes. As soon as the coin is considered to be firmly fixed, he takes away his hands, and also the coin. The person operated upon is then told to shake the sixpence down to the floor, without any aid from his hands, and so strong generally is the impression made upon the mind of the victim that the sixpence is still on the forehead, that the shaking may be continued for several minutes before the deception is discovered.

11. *Put one hand where the other cannot touch it.* This is done by merely holding the right elbow with the left hand.

12. *Kiss the candlestick.* Request a young lady to hold a lighted candle, and then steal a kiss from her.

13. *Laugh in one corner of the room, sing in another, cry in another, and dance in another.*

from *Cassell's Book of Indoor Amusements, Card Games and Fireside Fun*

Clubs and Pubs

The Fashionable Club

A modern London club is the very looking-glass of the time; of the gay, glittering, polished, improved utilitarian, material age. Nothing more can be done for a palace than the fitters-up of a modern club have done for it. The march of upholstering intellect is there in its entirety. It must be almost bewildering to the modest half-pay captain or the raw young ensign, to the country gentleman, the book-worm fellow of his college, or the son of the country squire, fresh from dog-breaking and superintending the drains on his father's estate, to find themselves suddenly transferred from the quiet lodgings in St Alban's Place, the whitewashed barrack-room, the ivy-grown parsonage, the tranquil oak-sporting rooms of "Keys" or "Maudlin," the dull comfort of the country mansion-house, to this great hectoring palace, of which he is the twelve-hundreth part proprietor, and where he may live on the fatness of the land, and like a lord of the creation, for twenty guineas entrance fee, and a subscription of ten guineas a year. He has a joint-stock proprietorship in all this splendour; in the lofty halls and vestibules; in the library, coffee-rooms, newspaper and card-rooms; in the secretary's office in the basement; and in the urbane secretary himself; in the kitchen, fitted with every means and appliance, every refinement of culinary splendour, and from whence are supplied to him at cost prices dishes that would make Lucullus wild with envy, and that are cooked for him, besides, by the great *chef* from Paris, Monsieur Nini Casserole, who has a piano and a picture-gallery in the kitchen—belongs, himself, to a club, little less aristocratic than his masters', and writes his bills of fare upon laced-edged note-paper. From the gorgeous footmen in plush and silk-covered calves, which the flunkeys of duchesses could scarcely rival, to the little foot-page in buttons; from the letter-racks to the French-polished peg on which he hangs his hat in the hall; from the books in the library to the silver spoons in the plate-basket; from the encaustic mosaic on the pavement of the hall to the topmost turreted chimney-pot—he has a vested interest in all. He cannot waste, he cannot alienate, it is true; he can but enjoy. Debentures have taken care of that; yet the fee-simple is in part his; he is the possessor of an entailed estate; yet, for all purposes of present enjoyment, he sits under his own roof on his own ground, and eats his own mutton off his own plate, with his own knife and fork. Oh! the wonderful workings of debentures, and the inestimable benefits they confer on genteel persons with expensive tastes and small incomes! Do you know that a man may drink wines at his club, such as, were he to order them at an hotel, the head waiter would hold up his hands at the extravagance of the order, or else imagine that he had Rothschild or Mr Roupell dining in No. 1 box; nay, might perchance run round to the chamber-maid to ask how much luggage the gentleman had. Rare ports, "worn-out ports", grown colourless from age and strength, that cannot be looked at without winking—wondrous bitter Sherries—strange yellow Rhine wines, that gurgle in the glass when poured out—Claret that has made bankrupt the proprietors of the *vignobles* who grew them, or else sent them mad to think their stock was out—in-describable Cognacs—Maraschinos and Curaçoas that filtrate like rich oil: all these are stored by special wine-merchants in the cellars of the club. The chief butler, himself a prince among the winepots, goes forth jauntily to crack sales, and purchases, standing, the collec-tions of cunning amateurs in wines. You shall smoke such cigars at a club as would make Senor Cabana himself wonder where they were purchased. Everything is of the best, and everything is cheap; only the terms are, as the cheap tailors say, "for ready money". Tick is the exception, not the rule, at a club; though there have been Irish members who have run goodly scores in their time with the cook and the waiter.

A man may, if he be so minded, make his club his home; living and lounging luxuriously, and grazing to his heart's content on the abundant club-house literature, and enjoying the conversation of club friends. Soap and towels, combs and hair-brushes, are provided in the lavatories; and there are even some clubs that have bed-rooms in their upper storeys, for the use of members. In those that are deficient in such sleeping accommodation, it is only necessary to have a tooth-brush and an attic in an adjacent bye-street; all the rest can be provided at the club. Thus it is that, in the present generation, has been created a type peculiar thereunto—the club-man. He is all of the club, and clubby. He is full of club matters, club gossip. He dabbles in club intrigues, belongs to certain club cliques, and takes part in club quarrels. No dinners are so good to him as the club dinners; he can read no journals but those he finds in the club news-paper-room; he writes his letters on the club paper, pops them into club envelopes, seals them with the club seal, and despatches them, if they are not intended for postage, by the club messengers. He is rather sorry that there is no club uniform. He would like, when he dies, to be buried in a club coffin, in the club cemetery, and to be fol-lowed to the grave by the club, with members of the committee as pall-bearers. As it is, when he has shuffled off this mortal coil, his name appears on a board among the list of "members deceased". That is his epitaph.

from *Twice Round the Clock* by George Augustus Sala

The Smoking Room of the Liberal Club

The London Chess Club

In the very heart of the City of London, under the shadows of the Bank and Royal Exchange, and but a step from Lombard street, the London Chess Club holds its daily sittings. Who would expect to find such an association in such a place? Is the quiet of the chess arena consonant with the hum of busy multitudes, hurrying to and fro in never-failing ardour after the yellow god? Are stocks and scrip and dividends allied to gambits and mates? Shall Lloyd's Capel Court and the Corn Exchange furnish supporters of Caïssa? Come along with me to Cornhill. Stop! This is Purssell's restaurant. We'll walk up stairs. This room on the first floor is devoted to billiards. Above it meets the Cosmopolitan Club, and on the third floor—out of reach of the noise below—is the famous old "London", of which every player of note during the past fifty years has either been a member or visitor.

It is between three and four o'clock in the afternoon, and the rooms of the Club present the usual appearance at that hour. In the right-hand corner we perceive the President, Mr Mongredieu, engaged in dire conflict with Mr Maude, to whom he has offered the advantage of Pawn and Move. Readers of the *Chess Players' Chronicle*, of the *Palamède*, and *La Régence*, have known Mr Mongredieu for long years past, as an amateur of first-rate force, who gets himself invariably into difficulties at the commencement of a game, by his unvanquishable contempt for book openings, but who comes out all right at last, by his masterly tactics in the middle of the contest. Possessed of a fund of native English humour, and a finished scholar withal, he keeps up a running fire of wit and anecdote throughout the game, in which the lookers-on join. By his side is Mr George Medley, the Secretary of the Club, whose name is also a "household word" to amateurs, he and Mr Mongredieu ranking as the strongest players of the association. The latter gentleman has run in for an hour's play from the Corn Exchange, being in fact one of those men who, before the knowledge of Political Economy had become diffused amongst the masses, were styled "the rogues in grain". Mr Medley has just arrived from the Stock Exchange, where, after "Bearing" or "Bulling" Mr Slous, George Walker, and Mr Waite during the morning, he meets them at the Chess Club towards three o'clock, and they become as much absorbed in the mysteries of the game as though it were the business of their lives.

If you wish to see what influence chess can have upon individuals, just analyze the London Club. The members are not "men of straw", but sound, substantial citizens, with balances at their bankers heavy enough to buy up half-a-dozen lords.

These are the men, the very men, who repealed the Corn Laws in 1846, established the principle of Free Trade, and told a proud, titled aristocracy—"We, the middle class, the merchants, bankers, and manufacturers of Great Britain, are the source of all power in England, as we are the source of her greatness."

An admirable demonstration of these ideas is to be found in the London Chess Club. This association has flourished with never-failing vigor since its establishment in 1807, whilst Clubs have risen, waned, and died at the fashionable end of the town. City men are too patriotic and too proud to allow their Club to languish; and, depend upon it, whilst the old London counts a single member, that one last man will, from his own purse, find funds to keep it alive, inscribe on his colours "*Lateat scintillula forsan*", and shout with stentorian lungs for recruits.

from *The Exploits and Triumphs in Europe of Paul Morphy, the Chess Champion* by Frederick Milne Edge

Nat Langham and the Rum-Pum-Pas

It is as the only conqueror of Tom Sayers that Nat Langham is best known to the present generation. And he never did a cleverer stroke of business than when he started his famous convivial and sporting club, the Rum-Pum-Pas. Mr John de Rougemont was the first president, and, in virtue of his office, was custodian of the records of the society.

The members used to meet on Wednesday evenings, and a novel feature of their gatherings was that they dined inside a regulation 24 ft square ring. It was a tremendous squeeze sometimes to get all the company crowded into that narrow space, but the tighter the fit the merrier the company.

The chief dish, for which the club was famous, was plum-pudding. Two of these puddings, one hot and the other cold, were regularly supplied by Mrs Burnell, of the King's Arms, Hanwell, who is still, I believe, living at Shepherd's Bush, where her husband is (or was) a noted canine doctor. These puddings that excellent cook sent off in good time every Wednesday, the warm one carefully wrapped in flannel, and standing on a hot-water plate, in charge of her husband, who, under the direst penalties, was enjoined to deliver them safe and sound at the Cambrian in time for the dinner.

They sat late, did these jovial Rum-Pum-Pas, and the artful Nat frequently beguiled them into an all-night session by promising them a merry little mill in the morning between two lads well matched in weight, age, and science, who were ready to fight at some secluded spot—usually down Epsom way—and were certain to show excellent sport.

After Nat Langham's death in 1871, the club removed its quarters to Alec Keene's, the Three Tuns, in Moor Street, Soho. It continued to hold its meetings until 1879; but as many of the old members had gone over to the majority, and those who remained had lost their zest for that kind of thing now that the Prize Ring was defunct, it was determined to wind up the institution with a final and farewell banquet.

There was a pretty good muster. Among those present were Mr Wilbraham, the three Joyces—Bill, Fred and Cocky—Alec Keene, Jem Ward, Phil Benjamin, Bill Burnell (with the two plum-puddings)

Jemmy Shaw and a few more of the right sort, who did their best to revive the memories of the palmy days of the R.P.P. and make the last of its gatherings an occasion to be looked back upon with feelings of pleasure rather than regret. And so the Rum-Pum-Pas, of their own act and deed, ceased to exist.

from *Famous Fights—Past and Present* edited by Harold Furniss

The Hard-up Club

Just before I left the Bench, I had a visit from Pellatt, with the news that he and another jolly old friend of mine had made a discovery of a place of rest suitable to our condition in life, which I must inform the reader was seedy in every respect.

Pellatt had been in the habit of coming over to the priory almost daily to dine with me and others who were delighted with his amusing qualities. He gave excellent imitations of the past and present London actors: his genius for entertaining was brought into active operation in our prison circle. The history of the discovery of the "nest", or tranquil house of retirement, was this:—Pellatt and Old Beans (whose right name, I should state, was Bennett, ycleped Beans for shortness) were strolling about the Strand one foggy night in November. Their habiliments were uncomfortably ventilated; their crabshells[1] of the order hydraulic;[2] snow was on the ground, and their castors "shocking bad hats". Not liking to enter any very public places, they strayed round the back streets on the river side of the Strand, and turning from Norfolk Street into Howard Street, *vis à vis* they perceived the identical tavern they were looking for—a dull, unlighted, save by a dim lamp, small, old-fashioned public-house in Arundel Street, the sign of the Swan.

"The Swan," said Pellatt, as he read the sign. "The Swan," he continued, "will never sink. Beans, old fellow, we'll go into the 'Never Sink'."

This was an emphatic baptism, sprinkled often afterwards from the chalice of gin and water. The house was better known for years afterwards as the "Never Sink" than by its real sign, "The Swan".

The two wayfarers entered. Old Charles Mathews, in his "at

home", used to tell a story of pulling up at a roadside inn, and interrogating the waiter as to what he could have for dinner.

"Any hot joint?" said the traveller.

"No, sir, no hot joint, sir."

"Any cold one?"

"Cold one, sir? No, sir, no cold one, sir."

"Can you broil me a fowl?"

"Fowl, sir? No, sir, no fowl, sir."

"No fowl, and in a country inn!" exclaimed Mathews. "Let me have some eggs and bacon."

"Eggs and bacon, sir?" said the waiter. "No eggs and bacon, sir."

"D—n it!" at length said the hungry traveller, "what have you got in the house?"

"An execution, sir," was the prompt response of the doleful waiter; and so it was at the Swan. When Pellatt and his friend entered the parlour there was but a glimmer of light, and no fire. A most civil man, whose name turned out to be Matthews, informed his guests that he would instantly light a fire, and make them comfortable.

"Not worth while," said Pellatt; "we only want a glass of gin and water and a pipe."

Mine host would not be denied. In a few minutes there was a blazing fire, the hot grog was on the table, and Pellatt and Old Beans were smoking away like steam. The host was invited to take a seat with them. He did so, and during their conversation informed them that he was the man in possession, and that he was allowed to provide a little spirits and a cask of beer, and reap the profits himself, just to keep the house open until a purchaser could be found for it; and he further stated how glad he should be if the gentlemen would come again. The fact was that, in that dull hole, as it might well be called, the poor fellow had been almost buried alive; and the sudden appearance of the witty and jocose individuals before him had enchanted him to the seventh heaven. He wanted them to stay all night. Being, by Pellatt, apprised of all this when I again left quod and visited the outer world, I aided them in establishing that which we dignified by the title of the "Hard-up Club". Its initiation commenced by Old Beans being appointed steward; and in that capacity he commenced his campaign by purchasing a pound of cold boiled beef at Cautis's, at Temple Bar, and four pennyworth of hot roasted potatoes from the man who stood with the baked "tatur" can in the front of St Clement's Inn. As our club increased in numbers, so did our commissariat in supplies and importance. The office of Old Beans became no sinecure. His duty—and it was performed *con amore*—was to be in attendance early in the day at the club, and provide the dinner, the money to pay for which was invariably collected overnight; and I have known the funds to be so short that Old Beans's ingenuity has been greatly taxed to meet the necessary requirements and expenditure. A shoulder of mutton was a familiar dish, Beans preparing heaps of potatoes, and with a skilful culinary nicety, for which he was eminent, making the onion sauce himself. A bullock's heart was also a favourite with us, provided always that Old Beans made the gravy and stuffing. I said to our gracious and economical steward, the first day we had the ox-heart, "Beany, you'll want some gravy-beef." "The deaf-ears,"[3] said he, scratching his own, "will make excellent gravy; the 'Hard-ups' can't afford beef, old fellow. No, no, the deaf-ears, old cock!"

The reader will intuitively imagine that Old Beans's place was a difficult one. One Kay, a large, seedy lawyer, who wore shabby black-and-white stockings and shoes, was always behindhand with his due share of cash. If a shilling was required, Kay would pay into the hands of the steward ninepence half-penny, vowing that he had no more. Beans always declared himself out of pocket by Kay. We had, however, a spirit which added lustre to our association. He was not, however, a dining member; he could not be—his means were too limited even for our humble carousings. This member was a very old man, Colonel Curry, formerly a member of the Irish Parliament. He lodged in one room in Arundel Street; therefore the "Never Sink" was to him a convenient hostelry, and he could do as he liked. He did so. On a small shelf over the parlour door the colonel kept his own table-napkin, mustard, pepper, and salt; he had a small, gravy-tight tin case made, and in that he brought with him every day a fourpenny plate of hot meat, invariably bought at a cook-shop at the corner of the yard of the Angel Inn, St Clement's. All he spent in the house was three-halfpence for a glass of rum, which he diluted from six o'clock in the evening till eleven o'clock at night: the last mixing the rum could not be recognised—the water was colourless. Curry was a proud Irishman: he never accepted the oft-proffered hospitality of others. His conversation was delightful, amusing, and instructive.

He never complained. We were left in doubt whether his economy proceeded from parsimony or poverty: from his highly honourable sentiments I should conclude the latter. It was a rule with the club that all the good sort of fellows with whom the members might be acquainted should be pressed into the general service of the club: thus any member who, in better days, had been a good customer to a thriving publican (and there was scarcely an exception in the whole society), should use his best endeavours to bring him to the "Never Sink", and get him to stand treat. The number of dinners and the gallons of lush obtained by these fair pretences, which are not recorded by their numerical amount, was, in the words of Dominie Sampson, PRODIGIOUS!

[1] A term—old shoes.
[2] Letting water.
[3] The hard gristly substance attached to the top of a bullock's heart.

from *Rogue's Progress* by Renton Nicholson

The interior of a Liverpool public house

I Likes a Drop of Good Beer

Come one and all, both great and small,
  With voices loud and clear,
And let us sing bless Billy the King
  Who bated the tax upon beer;

For I likes a drop of good beer, I do,
  I likes a drop of good beer;
And damn his eyes whoever tries
  To rob a poor man of his beer.

Let Ministers shape the duty on Cape,
  And cause Port Wine to be dear,
So that they keep the bread and meat cheap,
  And gi'e us a drop of good beer.

For I likes a drop, etc.

My wife and I feel always dry
  At market on Saturday night.
Then a noggin of beer, I never did fear,
  For my wife always says that it's right.

For she likes a drop, etc.

Long may Queen Victoria reign,
  And be to her subjects dear,
And wherever she goes we'll wallop her foes,
  Only give us a skinful of beer.

For we likes a drop, etc.

                                    Anon.

Saturday Night

... I must describe the way of paying wages on a Saturday night. We usually left the works between five and six o'clock. The custom was to pay three or four men, with their helpers, in one lump sum, say a five-pound note, and some odd sovereigns. It would have been just as easy for the employers to get silver or half-sovereigns, so that each worker could get his or her pay direct. No such thoughtful providence, however, existed. The wages were fastened up in one lump until loosened at some public house. Men and women and children had to go there for their wages. The publican took good care to be in no hurry in changing the money given him. Each one—man, woman and child—was expected to have a hot roll and cheese, to be paid for out of the wage to be received, however small the pittance. The roll and cheese were right enough, but the payment was arbitrary and unequal. Those rolls and cheese were devoured with rare gusto. Such shining crust, and such white flaky insides, were never seen in "cottage loaves". The eyes of the youngsters had a paradisiacal vision before them, and the coy hesitation with which the crust was broken, the first dainty nibblings at the cheese, lest roll and cheese should get small too soon, were most amusing. It was something like the play of a cat with a mouse before she devours it. The boys would hold out the remainders of roll and cheese to show how much each one had left, and he was considered the hero of the hour who could seem to be eating all the time, and yet be the last to finish. The lad who finished, impelled by the strength of his hunger, was regarded with ironical compassion, and he regarded himself as a sort of victim, but couldn't tell who had victimized him.

The men, of course, soon ate their portion of food, and began the drinking, which, with short intervals, would not cease perhaps till the following Tuesday night. As the drinking went on they became talkative and effusive. Boys and women would be asked to drink and pressed to drink. In the case of the boys this sometimes meant semi-intoxication before the wages were received. Boys, I know, have been sent home drunk with the miserable pittance of two or three shillings in their pockets for working a week. . . . Meantime the publican kept the change back. Apparently he was counting untold pound-piles of silver, and if asked for the change, replied he was getting on as fast as he could, and that other folks were before them. Not until he was assured of a fair return for his "change", or until he saw his adult customers were settled for a night's booze, did he bring out the change. This may be said for the publican's honesty, I never remember a dispute about the change being wrong. When all were paid, the women and boys were sent home, the night's booze properly set in, and towards ten o'clock, poor wretched women would appear and entreat their husbands to go home. When this failed, they pleaded for money, as they had not a penny with which to pay the week's bills or to provide for the morrow. . . .

extract from an old potter's autobiography from *Useful Toil*

At the "Wagon and Horses"

Fordlow might boast of its church, its school, its annual concert, and its quarterly penny reading, but the hamlet did not envy it these amenities, for it had its own social centre, warmer, more human, and altogether preferable, in the taproom of the "Wagon and Horses".

There the adult male population gathered every evening, to sip its half-pints, drop by drop, to make them last, and to discuss local events, wrangle over politics or farming methods, or to sing a few songs "to oblige".

It was an innocent gathering. None of them got drunk; they had not money enough, even with beer, and good beer, at two-pence a pint. Yet the parson preached from the pulpit against it, going so far on one occasion as to call it a den of iniquity. "'Tis a great pity he can't come an' see what it's like for his own self," said one of the older men on the way home from church. "Pity he can't mind his own business," retorted a younger one. While one of the ancients put in pacifically, "Well, 'tis his business, come to think on't. The man's paid to preach, an' he's got to find summat to preach against, stands to reason."

Only about half a dozen men held aloof from the circle and those were either known to "have religion", or suspected of being "close wi' their ha'pence".

The others went as a matter of course, appropriating their own special seats on settle or bench. It was as much their home as their own cottages, and far more homelike than many of them, with its roaring fire, red window curtains, and well-scoured pewter.

To spend their evenings there was, indeed, as the men argued, a saving, for, with no man in the house, the fire at home could be let die down and the rest of the family could go to bed when the room got cold. So the men's spending money was fixed at a shilling a week, sevenpence for the nightly half-pint and the balance for other expenses. An ounce of tobacco, Nigger Head brand, was bought for them by their wives with the groceries.

from *Lark Rise to Candleford* by Flora Thompson

The Costermongers' Free-and-easy

Every class in London has its particular pleasures. The gay have their theatres—the philanthropic their Exeter Hall—the wealthy their "ancient concerts"—the costermongers what they term their sing-song.

Just look at the people in this public-house. A more drunken, dissipated, wretched lot you never saw. There are one or two little tables in front of the bar and benches, and on these benches are the most wretched men and women possible to imagine. They are drinking gin and smoking, and all have the appearance of confirmed sots. They are shoemakers in the neighbourhood, and these women with them are their wives. "Lor' bless you, sir," exclaims the landlord, "they spend all they has in drink. They live on a penny roll and a ha'porth of sprats or mussels, and they never buy any clothes, except once in three or four years, and then they get some second-hand rubbish." And here, when they are not at work, they sit spending their money. . . . I know they are short-lived; I see in their pale, haggard, blotched, and bloated faces premature death. The first touch of illness will carry them off as rotten leaves fall in November. . . . But come upstairs into this concert-room, where about a hundred costermongers and shoemakers are listening to the charms of song. Talk about the refining influence of music! it is not here you will find such to be the case. The men and women and lads sitting round these shabby-looking tables have come here to drink, for that is their idea of enjoyment; and whilst we would not grudge them one particle of mirth, we cannot but regret that their standard of enjoyment should be so low. The landlord is in the chair, and a professional man presides at the piano. As to the songs, they are partly professional and partly by volunteers. I cannot say much for their character. The costermongers have not very strict notions of *meum* and *tuum*; they are not remarkable for keeping all the commandments; their reverence for the conventional ideas of decency and propriety is not very profound; their notions are not peculiarly polished or refined, nor is the language in which they are clothed, nor the mode in which they are uttered, such as would be recognised in Belgravia. Dickens makes Mrs General in "Little Dorrit" remark, "Society never forms opinions, and is never demonstrative." Well, the costermongers are the reverse of all this, and as the pots of heavy and the quarterns of juniper are freely quaffed, and the world and its cares are forgotten, and the company becomes hourly more noisy and hilarious, you will perceive the truth of my remarks. Anybody sings who likes; sometimes a man, sometimes a female, volunteers a performance, and I am sorry to say it is not the girls who sing the most delicate songs. The burdens of these songs are what you might expect. In one you were recommended not to go courting in the kitchen when the master was at home, but, instead, to choose the "airey". One song, with a chorus, was devoted to the deeds of "those handsome men, the French Grenadiers". Another recommended beer as a remedy for low spirits; and thus the harmony of the evening is continued till twelve, when the landlord closes his establishment, to the great grief of the few who have any money left, who would only be too happy to keep it up all night.

from *The Night Side of London* by J. Ewing Ritchie

C

Saturday Night

Of ham - mers and files no more heard the din is; Round the

door of the ware-house the work - men arr - ange, While the

mas - ter his bank - bills and snug lit - tle gui - neas Is

count - ing, or strut - ting a - bout to get change. Hav - ing

reck - oned they ne'er stop, but jog to the beer shop, Where

fumes of to - bac - co and sting - o in - vite, And the

o - ven in - hab - its a store of welsh rare - bits To

Chorus

feast jol - ly fel - lows on Sat - ur - day night. Sat - ur - day night boys,

Sat - ur - day night, What stir-rings in Shef-field on Sat - ur - day night.

Now while cheerful liquor around they are pushing,
The many-mouthed chorus melodious flies,
Though oft interrupted by merchants who rush in
With "Cockles alive O" or "Hot mutton pies".
Perhaps you may choose, sir, to pore o'er the news, sir,
And tell whether matters go wrong or go right:
All ranks and conditions commence politicians,
While sat in the alehouse on Saturday night.

But while o'er the tankard such fun they are raising,
Full often will fate these enjoyments annoy:
A good scolding wife puts her unwelcome face in;
An intruding guest, she breaks thus on their joy:
"So, here again, Billy, why, sure man, thou'rt silly;
'Od burn thee, come home, or I'll dit up thy sight."
"Nay, so now, my jewel," says he, "this is cruel,
To begrudge one a sup on a Saturday night."

Here maids with their baskets are to and fro walking
In shambles to bargain with butchers for meat,
While some boy ballad singer so slowly is stalking
And warbles so sweetly his lays in the street.
Here's calendars crying and people come buying,
Around the hoarse fellow in crowds—such a sight;
For, as suits your palates, confessions or ballads
Are all at your service on Saturday night.

When through the dark alleys, if slyly one passes,
What fun you may have if an ear you will lend:
Such sighs and soft wishes from lads and from lasses
Who tell their fond tale at a dark entry's end.
When he to his true-love cries, "Polly, adieu, love,"
And kisses and squeezes his lassie so tight,
She'll blushing say, "Fie, sir," then softly she'll cry, "Sir,
Can't you stay a bit longer, it's Saturday night?"

Anon.

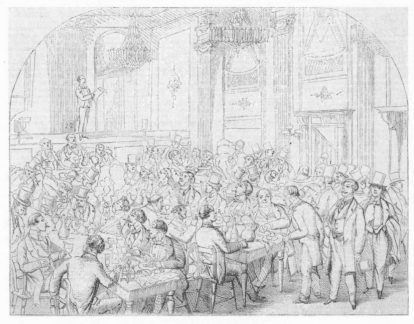

One a.m.—Evans's Supper-Rooms

One a.m.—Evans's Supper-Rooms

We require meat. So, says the friend most learned in the ways of the town to his companion—"Meat at our hotel we eschew, for we shall find the entertainment of the dearest and dullest. We will go sup at Evans's, for there we can have good meat and good liquor at fair rates, and hear a good song besides." Whereupon we walk till the piazza, about which I have kept you so long lingering, looms in sight. A low doorway, brilliantly lit with gas, greets our view. We descend a flight of some steps, pass through a vestibule, and enter the "Cave of Harmony".

Push further on, if you please. You are not to linger in this ante-chamber, thickly hung with pictures, and otherwise, with its circular marble tables, much resembling a Parisian *café*, minus the mirrors and the rattle of the dominoes.

Passing, then, through this *atrium*, the visitor finds himself in a

28

vast music-hall, of really noble proportions, and decorated not only with admirable taste, but with something nearly akin to splendour. You see I am at a loss for authorities again, and I cannot tell you how much of the hall is Corinthian, and how much composite; whether the columns are fluted, the cornices gilt or the soffits carved, and whether the Renaissance or the Arabesque style most prevails in the decorations employed. All I know is, that it is a lofty, handsome, comfortable room, whose acoustic properties, by the way, are far superior to those enjoyed by some establishments with loftier philharmonic pretensions. At the northern extremity of the hall is a spacious proscenium and stage, with the grand pianoforte *de rigueur*, the whole veiled by a curtain in the intervals of performance. As for the huge area stretching from the proscenium to a row of columns which separate it from the ante-chamber *café*, it is occupied by parallel lines of tables, which, if they do not groan beneath the weight of good eatables and drinkables piled upon them, might certainly be excused for groaning—to say nothing of shrieking, yelling, and uttering other lamentable noises, evoked by the unmerciful thumping and hammering they undergo at the conclusion of every fresh exercitation of harmony. . . .

But see the suppers set forth for the strong-stomached supporters of Evans's. See the pyramids of dishes arrive; the steaming succession of red-hot chops, with their brown, frizzling caudal appendages sobbing hot tears of passionate fat. See the serene kidneys unsubdued, though grilled, smiling though cooked, weltering proudly in their noble gravy, like warriors who have fallen upon the field of honour. See the hot yellow lava of the Welsh rabbit stream over and engulf the timid toast. Sniff the fragrant vapour of the corpulent sausage. Mark how the russet leathern-coated baked potato at first defies the knife, then gracefully cedes, and through a lengthened gash yields its farinaceous effervescence to the influence of butter and catsup. The only refreshments present open to even a suspicion of effeminacy are the poached eggs, glistening like suns in a firmament of willow-pattern plate; and those too, I am willing to believe, are only taken by country-gentlemen hard pressed by hunger, just to "stay their stomachs," while the more important chops and kidneys are being prepared. The clouds of pepper shaken out on these viands are enough to make Slawkenbergius sneeze for a fortnight; the catsup and strong sauces poured over them are sufficient to convince Sir Toby Belch that there are other things besides ginger, which are apt to be "hot i' the mouth," and, as humble servitors in attendance on these haughty meats, are unnumbered discs of butter, and manchets of crustiest bread galore.

Pints of stout, if you please, no puny half-measures, pints of sparkling pale ale, or creaming Scotch, or brownest Burton, moisten these sturdy rations. And when the strong men have supped, or rather before they have supped, and while they have supped, and indeed generally during the evening, there bursts out a strong smell of something good to drink; and presently you perceive that the strong men have ordered potent libations of spirituous liquors, hot whiskey-and-water being the favourite one; and are hastily brewing mighty jorums of punch and grog, which they undoubtedly quaff; puffing, meanwhile, cigars of potency and fragrance—pipes are tabooed—taken either from their own cigar-cases, or else recently laid in from the inexhaustible stores of the complaisant Herr von Joel.

from *Twice Round the Clock* by George Augustus Sala

The Judge and Jury Club

It is years since I was at a Judge and Jury Club, but I believe their character is in no degree changed. The one I speak of met in an hotel not far from Covent-garden, and was presided over by a man famous in his day for his power of *double entendre*. About nine o'clock in the evening, if you went up stairs you would find a large room with benches capable of accommodating, I should think, a hundred, or a hundred and fifty persons. This room was generally well filled, and by their appearance the audience was one you would call respectable. The entrance fee entitled you to refreshment, and that refreshment, in the shape of intoxicating liquor, was by that time before each visitant. After waiting a few minutes, a rustle at the entrance would cause you to turn your eyes in that direction, when, heralded by a crier with a gown and a staff of office, exclaiming, "Make way for my Lord Chief Baron," that illustrious individual would be seen wending his way to his appointed seat. The man I write of was then about thirty-five, but he appeared much older, and in his robes of office and with his judicial wig had almost a venerable appearance. Having seated himself and bowed to the bar, the Lord Chief Baron called for a cigar and glass of brandy and water, and, having observed that the waiter was in the room and that he hoped gentlemen would give their orders, the proceedings of the evening commenced. A jury was selected; the prosecutor opened his case, which, to suit the depraved taste of his patrons, was invariably one of seduction or crim. con. Witnesses were examined and cross-examined, the females being men dressed up in women's clothes, and everything was done that could be to pander to the lowest propensities of depraved humanity. I do not believe the audience could have stood this if it had not been for the drink. As it was, I believe many a youth fresh from home felt a little ashamed of himself that he should be in such company listening to such unmitigated ribaldry, but these reflections were soon drowned in the flowing bowl, and the lad, if he blushed at first, soon learned to laugh.

*   *   *   *   *

After the defence came the summing up, which men about town told you was a model of wit, but in which the wit bore but a small proportion to the obscenity. The jury were complimented on their intelligent and lascivious appearance, all the filthy particulars which had been noticed were referred to Dog Latin, and poetical quotations were plentifully thrown in; and by twelve, amidst the plaudits of the audience, the affair, so far as the Judge and Jury Club was concerned, was over. Then there was supper for such as wished it, and an entertainment to follow, either in the shape of a concert or of an exhibition of *Poses Plastiques*. To these subsequent entertainments ladies were generally admitted—and perhaps the less I say about them or their proceedings the better. If I refer to them at all, it is but as an illustration of the drinking customs of society. These Judge and Jury Clubs after all are but an excuse for drinking. They are held at public-houses—there is drinking going on all the time the trial lasts,—nor could sober men listen unless they had the drink.

*   *   *   *   *

If you wish to see your son thoroughly depraved, send him to a Judge and Jury Club. In a little while he will come back to you with every noble principle blotted out, with a mind stored with pollution, and with a fitting phraseology, ready to run a mad career of debauchery and vice. Some fifteen years back the writer was at college, and one of his fellow-students was a fine young fellow, the heir to a decent fortune, and said to be connected with a noble family. The last time I was at the Judge and Jury he was employed as one of the mock counsel; but he became too intemperate even for that, and enlisted, and miserably died. They have tragic ends, many of these frequenters of Judge and Jury Clubs, and it is sad to think that, when the merriment is the loudest, and the drink is most stimulating, and the fellowship most jovial, there is burlesque even then.

from *The Night Side of London* by J. Ewing Ritchie

A gin palace

The Eagle Tavern

Is situated in an appropriate locality in the City-road, not far from a lunatic asylum, and contiguous to a workhouse. From time immemorial the Cockneys have hastened thither to enjoy themselves. Children are taught to say—

> "Up and down the City-road,
> In and out the Eagle,
> That's the way the money goes,
> Pop goes the weasel."

And the apprentice or clerk, fresh from the country, and anxious to see life, generally commmences with a visit to the Grecian Saloon— Eagle Tavern. As a rule, I do not think what are termed fast men go much to theatres. To sit out a five-act tragedy and then a farce is a bore which only quiet old fogies and people of a domestic turn can endure; and even where, as in the Grecian Saloon, you have dancing, and singing, and drinking added, it is not the fast men, but the family parties, that make it pay.

*   *   *   *   *

I will call evidence as to the character of the amusements at the Eagle Tavern. In the parliamentary report on public-houses, I find Mr Balfour is examined respecting it. He says, "The most detrimental place of which I know, as far as women are concerned, is the Eagle Tavern in the City-road. There are gardens, and statues round the gardens, and everything to attract. There is a large theatre, and there are theatrical representations during the week. I have seen women there whom I have recognized next day as common street-walkers. The gardens are open, with alcoves and boxes on each side, and lads and young persons are taken in there and plied with drink. The house is opened on Sunday evening, but on Sunday evening there is no dramatic representation nor music. I have seen gentlemen come out drunk."

*   *   *   *   *

Now, Mr Conquest, the present proprietor, must have read all this evidence, yet I do not see that he has taken any steps to reform the evil complained of. It pays, I suppose, and that is enough. Much money has been made by it. The late proprietor retired a wealthy man. The present proprietor, we presume, trusts to do the same, and if the establishment panders to vice, if women date their ruin to Sunday evenings there, if mothers see their sons robbed of all that would make them decent men owing to their visits there, what's the odds? cries the dram-seller, who, like another Cain, asks if he be his brother's keeper.

The regular attendants see this not. "It's a beautiful place," says Mrs Smith to Mrs Robinson, "a'nt it, my dear?" as they sit eating questionable sausage rolls, and indulging in bottled beer. They see the pictures in the balcony, and think the gas jets quite miraculous, and admire the weak fountains and ambitious grottoes—and they laugh even at the comic singer, a feat I cannot achieve anyhow. Evidently the Eagle Tavern audience is of the same genus as an Adelphi audience, a people easily moved to laughter, and much given to taking their meals with them,—a people not prone to look before or after,—who would be drowned rather than get up and walk into the Ark, and who see no chance of their own house being burnt down in the fact that their neighbour's house is in flames. I don't believe naturally men or women are these dull clods, but custom makes them such, and they see no danger, nor perhaps is there where they are concerned. If there be no inner light, you cannot quench it; if the soul be dead, you need not wait for its trembling aspirations. Once within the vortex, it is in vain we warn: to the coming race, not to the race that has come, must we make our appeal.

from *The Night Side of London* by J. Ewing Ritchie

THE SUCCESS OF THE GAIETY BURLESQUE "MAZEPPA" WAS MISS BESSIE BELLWOOD'S SONG "WHAT CHEER 'RIA" SUNG BY MISS NELLY FARREN. *Vide Press.*

"WHAT CHEER 'RIA"

WRITTEN BY
WILL HERBERT
COMPOSED & SUNG WITH ENORMOUS SUCCESS BY
BESSIE BELLWOOD.

PROFESSIONAL VOCALISTS MAY NOT SING THIS SONG IN PUBLIC WITHOUT MISS BESSIE BELLWOOD'S PERMISSION.

LONDON: HOPWOOD & CREW, 42, NEW BOND ST W.

Wotcher 'Ria

I am a girl what's-a-do-ing we-ry well in the we-ge-ta-ble line, And as I'd sav'd a bob or two, I

thought I'd cut a shine. So I goes and buys some togger·y, These 'ere

we·ry clothes you see, And with the mon·ey I had left I

thought I'd have a spree. So I goes in·to a mus·ic hall where I'd

oft·en been a·fore, I don't go in the gal·ler·y but on the bot·tom

floor; I sits down by the Chair·man and calls for a pot of

Stout, My pals in the gal·ler·y spot·ted me, and they

Chorus

all com·menced to shout. Wot·cher 'Ri·a? 'Ri·a's on the

job, Wot·cher 'Ri·a? Did you spec·u·late a

bob? Oh, 'Ri·a she's a toff and she looks im·men·si·

koff, And they all shout·ed, Wot·cher 'Ri·a?

36

Of course I chaffed them back again, but it worn't a bit of use.
The poor old Chairman's baldie head they treated with abuse;
They threw an orange down at me, it went bang inside a pot,
The beer went up like a fountain, and a toff copt all the lot;
It went slap in his chevy, and it made an awful mess,
But what gave me the needle was, it spoilt me blooming dress.
I thought it was getting rather warm, so I goes towards the door,
When a man shoves out his gammy leg, and I fell smack on the
    floor.

SPOKEN: *I turned round and spoke to him wery politely. I said, "What
cher want to go and shove your jolly old gammy leg out like that for?"
He said, "I beg your pardon, Madam." I says, "Beg nothing, you jolly
old josser!" He says, "Don't you be saucy or I shall get you chucked
out." When my pals spot I'm having a row, and they see the old man has
got a wooden leg, they shout out, "Wotcher! Half a man and half a
tree?!"*

Chorus

Now the gent that keeps the Music Hall he patters to the bloke,
Of course they blamed it all on me, but I couldn't see the joke.
So I upped and told the governor as how he'd shoved me down,
And with his jolly old wooden leg, tore the frilling off my gown.
But law bless you! It worn't a bit of use, the toff was on the job.
They said, "Outside!" and out I went, and they stuck to my bob.
Of course I left so wild, to think how I'd been taken down,
Next time I'll go in the gallery with my pals, you bet a crown.

SPOKEN: *You don't catch me going chucking my money away, trying to
be a toff any more—the way they served me wasn't so very polite. They
brought the chucker-out and he said, "Come on, 'Ria, you've been kicking
up a pretty row," he says, "Come on, outside." I says, "Shan't, shan't!
There you are! Shan't!!" He took hold of me and handed me out, just
as though I'd been a sack of taters. When I got outside, my young man
was waiting. So he says, "Serves you jolly well right, 'Ria! You
shouldn't try to be a lady, 'cause it don't suit yer." Just then my pals
were coming out of the gallery and they all commenced shouting:*

Chorus

Dan Leno

Dan Leno

Dan Leno! The acknowledged king of comedians. Clearly I recall the little man when, in 1885, he first appeared at the famous hall in Piccadilly Circus. After his début at the Middlesex, the same year, his rise to fame was meteoric. He was hailed as a comic genius. Over a span of twenty years I heard Leno sing, as I believe, every character song in his extensive repertoire. The early ditties were not so irresistibly funny as those gems he gave us in later years. Dan depended on his patter, the singing being negligible. On the halls, his range of characters was both wide and varied. I recall seeing him as many kinds of henpecked husband, several dames, a railway guard, a recruiting sergeant, a shopwalker ("Walk this way, step this way"), a Japanese, a Beefeater, a Highland Chieftain, a Doctor, a Waiter, a Grocer's Assistant, a Tower Warden, and several others. How we roared with laughter when the wee fellow began to explain to us, how he went about "courting the widow," and how, when passing his chair, the lady would playfully drop some red-hot cinders down his back. "All those little tricks tell, you know!" said Dan. "There was no mistaking her meaning. It was love at second sight." And it was also a joy to hear him discoursing on Mrs Kelly. ("You know Mrs Kelly, surely? You should—you *must* know Mrs Kelly. Don't say no. You are *bound* to know Mrs Kelly.") There was, too, his dissertation on eggs. ("There are two kinds of eggs, fresh and election eggs. Then, there is *the* egg.") Again, as a Huntsman, when his horse lost its way, and, wandering into the farmyard, put its feet into a dung-heap. "Oh," said Dan, "It was quite easy to follow the scent for miles, and then, it followed *me*, all the way home." Another Leno laugh was his skit "Buying a House", when he admitted that, "although the river was at the bottom of the garden, sometimes the garden was at the bottom of the river."

Then he sent us into ecstasies when he expounded his theory as to how and when and why the "Minstrel Boy" did this, that, and the other, and, the reason for having his harp hung, flung, or slung behind him. On another occasion, Dan, in the middle of a song, would suddenly stop singing, and, taking off his hat, he would inspect it all over. "That's not *my* hat," he cried. "That's *never* my hat. Very strange. I came here to-night wearing a different one to this." And then, indignantly, he would toss the offending headgear into the wings, give a double shuffle, and resume his interrupted song. But there were other choice tit-bits in Leno's fun menu. He would commence a Scotch ditty anent MacDougal's men, MacPherson's men, MacLaglan's men, and one other Caledonian warrior. Of a sudden he would "dry up," smite his forehead, and gaze upwards, as if trying to recollect the name of the fourth member. He would start all over again, with the same result. "It's no use," said Dan, "I'm terribly sorry, but, I can't remember the name of the other Mac! Never mind. Play a horn-pipe, professor" (to the conductor), and, away he would go, dancing madly up and down the stage, amid shrieks and yells and screams from the audience until, giving a sudden shout of triumph, he stopped. "I've got it," he cried, "I've got it. MacGoggle's men. That's it—MacGoggle's men. I knew the name would come back to me!" And, delighted with his success, the little man would skip off the stage amid a hurricane of applause, to be recalled again and again.

from *The Performer*, Christmas 1956

39

MIDDLESEX
MUSIC HALL, DRURY LANE.
Proprietor. ....MR. H. R. LANE.   Managing Director ... MR. HARRY FOX

THE NIGHT OF TALENT, WONDER & DELIGHT
IN SET APART FOR THE FIRST COMPLIMENTARY

BENEFIT
TO

Mdme. PLEON
GEN. TOM DOT & MAJOR MITE
WEDNESDAY, March 12, 1872.

GEO. FREDERICKS & CARRIE JULIAN
The Greatest Duettists of the Period.

FRED COYNE
The Great Comic.

FRED ALBERT
The Great Topical Vocalist, Author and Composer

FOTHERGILL & SUMMERSON
The Celebrated Comic Vocalist.

Mr. ALF. WALKER
The People's Comic.

EDWARD MOSEDALE
The great Nautical and Patriotic Vocalist.

MR. W. BAKER
The Favorite Serio-Comic.

MISS KATE MACNAMARA
The great Provincial Serio-Comic.

MISS LIZZIE GRAHAM
The Talented Character Singer and Dancer.

MISS LOUISE PATTIE
(Five in number).

THE DE CASTRO FAMILY, MALE & FEMALE ACROBATS,

YOUNG ENGLAND & LITTLE ALFRED
On the High Trapeze.

* THE GREAT EVENT ! *
MR. HARRY FOX & **MDME. PLEON**
Mr. HARRY FOX will also sing "Jolly Nose"; in this song he has no rival.

THE WONDROUS TWO-HEADED SKYLARK
Will positively appear for this night only.

MISS JULIA HARTRIDGE
Serio-Comic.

HARRY WINGETT
Comic. "Have you seen my Uncle Benjamin?"

W. T. CRITCHFIELD
Versatile Comic.

PROF. PETERSON'S TROUPE OF PERFORMING DOGS.

HARRY SEFTON
The Dancing Spider.

The Charming SISTERS LINDON
Scotch Vocalist and Dancer.

JESSIE DANVERS
The great Ventriloquist.

LIEUTENANT COLE
Serio-Comic.

MISS AGNES RAYMOND
The greatest Negro Comedian of the age.

CHARLES FOX & LAURA SEDGWICK

Master PERCY PLEON
The Smallest and Youngest Drummer in the world.

Madame PLEON
Will sing her celebrated Swiss Songs.

General TOM DOT & Major MITE

SIR ROWLAND THE VILLAIN !
Or, THE POOR BUT VIRTUOUS VILLAGE MAID.

The Night of Excitement! Night of Amusement! Night of Grand Entertainment!

WEDNESDAY, March 12.

Reserved Stalls or Balcony, 1s. Lower Hall or Balcony, 6d.
J. W. LAST & Co., Printers, Ivinson Street, Drury Lane, W.C.

MIDDLESEX
MUSIC HALL,
THE MOGUL, DRURY LANE, LONDON.
Proprietor and Manager · · · Mr. J. L. GRAYDON.

Monster Variety Company.
LIGHTNING PROGRAMME.

MONDAY, NOVEMBER 23rd, 1891,
AND EVERY EVENING.

The Inimitable Vocal and Patter Comedian,

DAN LENO
IN ALL HIS LATEST SUCCESSES,
Again at the Middlesex, the home of his early triumphs.

ALICE CONWAY
AND
ED. CLARK,
In their American Variety and Song and Dance Entertainment.

RETURN OF
G. H.
CHIRGWIN
The Original and only White-Eyed Kaffir.

LOMBARDO & JEFFS, Musical Clowns.
PATTIE THORNHILL, Serio and Dancer.
VICTOR VERNON, Comedian.
SISTERS LA MARA, Duettists.

PAT RAFFERTY,
The Favourite Character-Comedian.

WALTON & LESTER,
Eccentric Comedians.

Return of the Middlesex Favourites
BOB & JENNY LEONNARD,
Just from America.

The Popular Serio-Comic Artiste
NELLY L'ESTRANGE
"THE POOR GIRL DIDN'T KNOW, YOU KNOW."

CORBETT AND MYERS. | **MEADOWS AND ACTON.**

PROFESSOR PETERSON
AND HIS TROUPE OF EDUCATED DOGS.

The New Comedian
GEORGE ROBY,
In his Latest Successful Songs.

CHAIRMAN · · MR. ALFRED ROBERTS.
A CHANGE EVERY WEEK.
FEWTRELL & Co., Printers, 36 Leigh Queen Street, High Holborn, W.C.

Walking in the Zoo

(*Sung in the Music Halls by the Great Vance*)

The Stilton, sir, the cheese, the O.K. thing to do,
On Sunday afternoon, is to toddle to the Zoo;
Week days may do for cads, but not for me and you,
So dress'd, right down the road we show them who is who.

Walking in the Zoo, walking in the Zoo,
The O.K. thing on Sunday is walking in the Zoo.

So when there came to town my pretty cousin Loo,
I took her off to spend a Sunday at the Zoo;
I showed her the aquarium, the Tiger, the Zebu,
The Elephant, the Eland, that cuss—the Kangaroo.

Oh! walking in the Zoo, walking in the Zoo,
The monkeys put us to the blush on Sunday at the Zoo.

So into the monkey house, going in to woo,
Piling up the agony, swearing to be true,
Agony, indeed, for the cheerful cockatoo
Caught my ear a nip and bit it through and through.

Oh! that cheerful cockatoo, that awful cockatoo,
The horror and the agony, that Sunday in the Zoo.

Anon.

A Visit to the Zoological Gardens

We did not see much of the animals for the gentlemen were all so
very much fatigued that they sank down on some seats opposite the
elephants and there remained until near dinner time. I was very glad
that they rested themselves in front of a decent animal, for some of
them are very indelicate; indeed the monkeys are so very nasty that
I told Thomas Hawes I would rather not look at them—really, with
a gentleman, I think it quite indelicate.

extract from the diary of Fanny Horsley from
Leisure and Pleasure in the 19th Century

Wombwell's Menagerie

Tuesday 7 May 1872:   Wombwell's Menagerie came into Hay from Brecon Fair today and the elephant was advertised to ride upon a bicycle. This elephant is said to have killed a boy at the Potteries, but whether he did it by driving the bicycle over him or not did not appear. I went over to see the show but it was very late in coming into Hay. Someone said, the elephant had turned rusty on the road. Teddy Bevan and I went out to meet the caravans which were looming in the distance along the Brecon Road between the trees. The elephant, a very small one, and three camels or dromedaries came shuffling and splashing along the muddy road in heavy rain looking cold and miserable and shivering as if they were wet through. The camels were being towed by the caravans. The elephant walked very fast by the side. I noticed that the camels as well as the elephant moved both legs on one side at once. The camels were immediately put into the stable at the Blue Boar and I heard the owner or manager of the menagerie say to the ostler, "Get a wisp of straw and rub those camels down, they won't hurt you, they're as quiet as sheep." The wild beasts naturally put up at the Blue Boar. The show was advertised to take place at 3.30, but the beasts did not arrive till 4 and could not be shown till 6. . . .

At 6 o'clock the wild beasts were ready and we all went to the show. There was a fair lion and a decent wolf, which looked as if it had been just freshly caught, his coat was so thick and good and he was so strong and restless. A laughing hyena set us all off laughing in chorus. A black sheep in the pangs of hunger was bleating piteously and had forced his body half through the bars of his cage to get at the biscuits the children were offering him. The exhibition was small and poor. A dwarf three feet nothing pointed out to us "groups of wolves", stirred the beasts up with a long pole and made them roar. There was no bicycle forthcoming. The elephant did not get upon it or seem likely to do so. The camels were coming but not come.

The ground was in a swamp with pools of water and huge gaps in the canvas overhead let in the pouring rain. I soon went away. . . .

from *Kilvert's Diary* by Rev. Francis Kilvert

My First Circus

With the spring our circus was in a fair way of completion, and I resolved to open at King's Lynn at the great Charter Fair, which always commenced on February 14th, and lasted six days. So down to the grand old town on the east bank of the Ouse we made our way, and put up the new show, with its pictures illustrating the greatest impossibilities it is possible to conceive.

But they served their turn admirably, and when we—that is to say, myself; my nieces, nephew, and apprentices; Watty Hilyard, the famous clown; John Croueste, the noted general performer; and William Kite, who came of a wonderful circus family, and could do almost any ring business you could mention—strutted forth before the public gaze, in tights and trunks, everybody, including even the showmen, was impressed and astonished.

I had bought for eighteen pounds another good horse, which was ridden from London to Norwich by Croueste, and we had trained it to gallop circus fashion in a proper forty-two feet ring in the public-house yard. All the time the fair lasted we were practising when not performing, and we speedily became very proficient.

We made money at King's Lynn, and, what was better, went on making it at the fairs we took in the Lincoln, Cambridge, Norfolk, and Suffolk district, while we were waiting for the great Eastertide Fair at Norwich. At this time, remember, our prices were a penny admission, with threepence for reserved seats.

On our way to Norwich Fair at Long Sutton, a mere village, we did what is known in the profession as "Blank Moulding". On a wide space in the turnpike road we put down a few seats and something in the shape of a ring, made up a few of the old-fashioned grease-pot lights with tallow and rags for wicks, and announced a grand performance. There was no charge to view the latter . . . but we charged a penny each to all who wanted a seat.

We presented a lively little programme of juggling, rope-walking, trick-riding, etc., and when half-way through it, in order to get our expenses, called a rest, during which the following bit of patter was indulged in: "Now, ladies and gentlemen, you know we are not doing this for our own amusement, but we thought as we were resting here to-night we would give you a little enjoyment. In order to test your appreciation of our efforts, before we go on with the rest of the performance the young men will go round with the hat." This is known in the profession as "nobbing", and not a soul among the spectators, some two or three hundred, escaped being "nobbed", whether they parted or not. Then the second part of the performance proceeded.

The last item was my fortune-telling pony, who did very well until I came to the finish. This always was to tell the pony to go round and find out the biggest rogue in the company. The proper response was to walk up to the ringmaster, so pointing him out as the biggest rogue in question. I never knew him do a wrong thing before, but on this occasion, after I had given him his order, and stood with my back to him waiting for him to come and push his head against me, I heard the people laughing.

Turning round, I saw the pony with his head resting on the shoulder of the village constable, who looked very red and unhappy. I at once threw the whip forward, driving the pony round the ring, at the same time saying, "You have made a mistake, sir! I told you to find the biggest rogue in the company: try again!" and with this I gave him the usual cue.

But it was of no use. The pony, instead of coming up to me, merely walked some ten paces on, then turned and came back to the unfortunate constable, while the crowd shrieked with laughter. I was now really vexed, so I cracked the whip, and the pony came up to me, while I said, giving him the knee cue, "You have been very rude to that gentleman; down on your knees, sir, to beg pardon for your mistake." But the crowd wouldn't have it. "No, no," they shouted; "pony knows better than you! Pony's all right! He made no mistake, he didn't! Us know pleeceman, and so do pony, it appears!" Here the laughter and the jeering broke out afresh, and we had to leave the matter where it stood.

The constable, however, was a very good fellow, and he came in with the rest afterwards and made a joke of it, for we had quite a gala night in the village, myself and company sitting among our patrons drinking four ale and smoking long pipes. The collection was a very good one, too; in fact, our bit of "blank moulding" quite paid expenses, besides making us some new friends, and giving us an excellent advertisement.

from *Seventy Years a Showman* by "Lord" George Sanger

Astley's

12 October 1844: . . . I went to Astley's Amphitheatre—I believe my chief motive was curiosity—To compare the building not seen since the fire—with Franconis at Paris—It is infinitely inferior and I cannot comprehend the blindness that prevented the adoption of the French form—which is worth the whole exhibition. The riding too appears to me infinitely inferior below that in Paris—at least there is nothing like *The Life of a French Soldier* which I felt to be deeply pathetic—there were two Melodramatic Exhibitions on the stage. One *Mazeppa* —there was effect produced in the Third act representing Mazeppa bound naked to the wild horse which carries him to Tarlazy where he is discovered to be the King's son—all the rest, his return to Poland and recovery, his Mistress included, vulgar enough. The other piece also as bad as possible—*The French at Morocco*—but for one striking portion—the Arab Chief performs the feats of Van Amberg. And we see him in the den with a Lion, Lioness, Tyger Leopard and this is a frightful exhibition and really worth the money. . . .

from *The London Theatre, 1811–66* by Henry Crabb Robinson

Cremorne Gardens

Towards eleven we went to Cremorne Gardens, where the day's madness was carried on far into the night. A crush and much shoving at the entrance; a gang of Englishmen crashed through shouting, "Make way for the Japanese Ambassadors!" Inside, especially at crossings in the walks, the press of people was dreadful, but it was possible to get a breath of air in the darker corners. All the men well or at least neatly dressed: the women were prostitutes but of a higher rank than those in the Strand; light-coloured shawls over white gauze or tulle dresses, red *mantelets*, new hats. Some of their dresses may have cost as much as £12. But the faces are rather faded and sometimes, in the crowd, they utter shocking screams, shrill as a screech-owl.

The most comical part, and which showed the degree of excitement, was the way they had of pinching people, especially foreigners. One of our party, a man past forty, having been thoroughly pinched, and even more thoroughly upset and offended, left the place. A woman rushed at a man who had trodden on her toes, and punched him in the back: he laughed and the whole crowd was delighted. They are certainly very good-natured; nobody lost their temper although there was good reason to, for one of our French friends was imprudently jeering and making fun of them out loud.

We sat down near three young women at a secluded table and offered them sherry and beer. They drank moderately. Our bookish English and their racy speech collided in a grotesque babel. One of them was very gay and wild: I have never seen such overflowing animal spirits. Another, modest, quite pretty, rather subdued, was a milliner by trade, entirely dependent on herself. She has a friend (lover) who spends his Sundays with her. I looked at her carefully; it was clear that she had the makings of an amiable and respectable girl. What had been the turning point?

from *Notes on England, 1860–70* by Hippolyte Taine

The Jenny Lind Mania

(Broadsheet published by E. Hodges, from Pitts, Wholesale Toy and Marble Warehouse, 31 Dudley Street, Seven Dials)

Oh! is there not a pretty fuss,
    In London all around,
About the Swedish Nightingale,
    The talk of all the town.
Each Square and Street as through you pass,
    Aloud with praises ring,
About this pretty singing bird,
    The famous Jenny Lind.

Chorus   For she turns each heart, and turns each head,
    Of those who hear her sing.
And she is turning all her notes to gold,
    Is famous Jenny Lind.

All singers she outshines,
    None can with her come nigh.
And some declares that she must be,
    An angel from the sky,
She sings so sweet, and sings so loud,
    As I've heard people say,
You might hear her from the Haymarket,
    As far as Botany Bay.

Chorus

As to a liquor shop you go,
    To drink your wine or gin,
The Landlord begs that you will taste
    His famous Jenny Lind,
And I heard a dustman t'other day,
    As he his bell did ring,
Instead of bawling out 'Dust O!'
    Called out for Jenny Lind.

Chorus

P—A—and our loving Queen,
    Had such a precious row
Because he at the Opera House
    To Jenny Lind did bow,
She beat him round and round the house,
    All with the rolling pin
Till he said, my dear, I will not look,
    Or wink at Jenny Lind.

Chorus

Anon.

November 3, 1848: . . . in the evening I went to the Theatre to hear Jenny Lind in the *Filgia del Reggimento*. I was in the gallery stalls where I could hear better than I could see—I had very little pleasure from her performance. I believe that in another piece I should have had more—I have no relish for high notes and military and gay musick abounds in these. I could recognize her marvellous power—her *shakes* are said to be wonderful—they may be—but that matters not—Once or twice there were soft and tender passages which I felt—came home late.

from The London Theatre 1811–66 by Henry Crabb Robinson

Rehearsing for a pantomime

Tableaux Vivants

The Theatrical Intelligence condemned at Drury Lane "as against public morality" . . . the Tableaux Vivants, or living statues, as they are somewhat absurdly called, which have night after night been allowed to pollute those boards once trodden by a Garrick and a Kemble. Where, we ask, in the name of common decency are these things to end? Are we to calmly suffer our mothers or our sisters to sit and witness human figures—but one remove from a state of nudity—standing in positions which, if represented by the artist's skill, would justly call down a prosecution from the Society for the Suppression of Vice? Are French *filles de joies*—our English phrase, though more expressive, is less decorous—to exhibit themselves in a manner equally repulsive and disgusting to the gaze of a British public?"

from *The Daily Despatch*

Pantomime at Drury Lane

Miss P. and two young Gents. going to the play (at) Drury Lane. The old Lady treated me to see it. The first part was *Sinderella*. I saw her in the kitchen among the sinders and saw the old wich turne her into a lady and made a carriage out of a pumpkin, four horses out of white mice, a coachman out of a rat, two footmen out of grasshoppers. This was done by the stage opening and the real things being pushed up by people below and the rat, mice and pumpkins and things being pulled below at the same time. Saw Sinderella go to the ball and lose her slipper and in the end was married to a Prince. The second part was a pantomime, where the clowns and harlaquins made a great deal of funn by turning one thing into another, such as an old woman into a young one and turning a publick house into a watermill. In this part I saw the Devil in hell. The place looked very firey and hot— not anything at all tempting. There were more things to numerous to mention. Got to bed by one o'clock.

extract from the diary of William Taylor, footman, from *Useful Toil*

When I Performed Othello!

All you who are disciples of Melpomene or Thespis,
I'll tell you of some sprees, if I may on your notice trespass;
My first appearance once I made, and my last, too, let me tell, O—
I never shall forget the night when I performed Othello.

I thought of acting I knew much, and none could reach fame
    swifter,
Because I knew a man that knew a Drury Lane scene shifter;
My face was black'd, the curtain rose—I came on such a gill, O!
'Cause I forgot to black my hands when I perform'd Othello!

I reach'd the lights, and made my bow, when those low gallery
    blackguards,
A rotten orange flung at me, which nearly knocked me backwards,
I reeled about, at length pitch'd into the orchestra pell mell, O!
And stuck fast in the double drum, when I perform'd Othello!

The actors, ever ripe for fun, thought me to make a butt on,
So instead of burnt cork made me rub my face with grease and soot
    on!
When Desdemona I embrac'd, oh, lud! how I did bellow,
For I daubed her cheeks all o'er with black, when I perform'd
    Othello!

At length, when order was restored, in spite of all my blunders,
I ranted, and I strutted, till I drew applause in thunders;
But when the house was all in tears, in the pit gets up a fellow,
And ask'd me if I'd sing "Jim Crow", when I perform'd Othello!

All else went smoothly till the scene where Desdemona's sleeping,
And entering with the lamp, the Moor towards the bed is
    creeping—
I somehow set the sheets alight, and horrible to tell O,
Poor Desdemona was burnt to death, when I perform'd Othello!

At length, when I approach'd the end, and all like babes were
    crying,
I somehow seem'd to gain fresh life when I commenc'd my dying;
En masse the audience rose, and each "encore!" did bellow—
So, to please 'em I died over again, when I perform'd Othello!

Sweeney Todd, the Demon Barber
(at the Royal Britannia Theatre, Hoxton)

An evening at the Britannia during the run of *The String of Pearls*; or, *The Barber Fiend of Fleet Street*, was to sup full of horror. In the vulgar tongue of Hoxton and elsewhere, a full supper is called a "tightener". The expression is coarse, no doubt, yet suggestive. Abominably so. Going to see *The Barber Fiend* was a tightener of horrors, like a visit to the small room at Madame Tussaud's.

The proceedings on the stage, of a midnight assassin who finds his victim asleep, are inscrutable. He looks at him—starts—recoils— then turns to the audience, and in a whisper fraught with tremendous significance puts them in possession of a circumstance which they have already had abundant opportunity of observing for themselves, namely, that "he sleeps!" He then proceeds to execute a series of brisk, but elaborate, manoeuvres about the stage, comprising a body of tactics sufficient to carry a small army through an ordinary campaign. I have never enjoyed the advantage of witnessing the perpetration of a murder off the stage, but it would seem to be unlikely that when such transactions take place in real life they are attended by the complicated evolutions above described. They correspond in point of eccentricity to the funny things which some people do on receiving a letter whose contents they are dying to know. They contemplate it externally in every possible point of view, and the aspect which it presents when held topsy turvy would appear to be a source to them of the most animated interest. It is subjected to a protracted course of manipulation, and in the process is done everything in the world to but read.

The consummation of the tragical situation at the R B is usually intensified by the tune of "a drop of good beer", played pensively. Objections might possibly be made by tiresome rigorists to the adoption of so genial and festive an air as an accompaniment to proceedings partaking in no way of a convivial spirit. But those who resort to a theatre in a mean and grudging spirit of petty captiousness are in no proper frame of mind for appreciating the pathetic and touching effects which the management have an eye to. For my own part, I can conscientiously affirm, in the conventional kind of language used by speakers at public dinners, that on one of these occasions "my emotions are of such a character as to be unlike anything which they do not resemble".

It is desirable that the practice adopted by Hoxton mothers of taking their babies to the theatre should be discontinued. The small miserables are brought out at the end of the evening with their feathers all rumpled, and their poor little eyes all glazed and fishy like those of old debauchees. Their general effect, too, conveys the impression of their having been sat upon, and otherwise exposed to gross personal contumely.

In the Biglow papers, some slaveholder or other talks of wishing to purchase "a low-priced baby" to bring up. Some of these embryo members of the R B public could only, if offered for sale, be got off at a wretchedly low figure, as damaged articles. Besides, too, their own personal sufferings, they are very undesirable neighbours to sit by. For, in the first place, they are apt to be—well—I forbear to press the details with unpleasant explicitness, and will therefore only say, in general terms—damp.

Very different from the condition of the poor babies is that of the youths in the gallery, who are gifted with a flow of exuberant animal spirits which find a safety-valve in shrill whistlings. . . .

Since the temperature up in their sixpenny heaven is so high (there was a fat little boy up there who I thought would have been melted and had to be taken home in a gallipot), they find it "cool and convanient" to sit without their coats. They evince, too, a noble independence of bearing and sentiment towards the swells in the body of the house (who are in this case the counter-skippers of Kingsland and Dalston) by turning their backs to the chandelier, and sitting along the gallery rail like a row of sparrows on a telegraph wire. In this position they confront their friends in the back settlements, and exchange with them a light fussillade of *badinage*, principally couched in idiomatic expressions of remarkable vigour and terseness, which is sustained with much animation during the time that the curtain is down between the pieces.

from *Letters from a Theatrical Scene Painter* by Thomas W. Erle

Dorkin's Night

'Twas Dorkin's night, and the house was a sight,
    It was packed from the floor to the roof;
His old friends were there, as they annually were
    When their friendship was put to the proof;
And the welcoming shout, which from thousands rang out,
    As their favourite came to the wing,
Convinced him he still could command them at will,
    And their laughter or tears could bring.

    But they knew not the pain in the poor player's breast
        As he strutted and mimicked and smiled;
    That while from his lips fell the mirth-giving jest,
        He thought of his poor dying child.

The first act was o'er and a deafening roar
    Of cheering went heartily round;
The second act passed, but alas! in the last,
    Dorkin scarcely could utter a sound;
They saw with dismay he was spoiling the play,
    It was plain there was something amiss;
And the unfeeling wit of the gods and the pit
    Came at last to a palpable hiss.

He started! turned pale, and his form seemed to quail,
    But he came to the footlights and spoke;
And the listening house was as still as a mouse,
    When the silence he falt'ringly broke;
"My little one's dead; I had left him in bed,
    Nearly gone when this drama began;
Yet I hoped he would live. You will surely forgive,
    For an actor can be but a man."

                                    Anon.

Henry Irving Begins His Theatrical Career

EDINBURGH,
February 23, '57.

MY DEAR MRS WILKINS,

My theatrical career commenced under the name of Henry Irving on the 29th September '56 at the opening of the Lyceum Theatre, Sunderland, in Durham, where I remained until the close of the season (a short one) which ended the 2nd inst. I was considered unusually successful for a first engagement, playing responsible (of course not leading) parts throughout the season. Miss Glyn was with us a fortnight; I thought of the days when I first heard her, and how changed are circumstances since then. Through the kind introduction and recommendation of our principal actor I obtained an engagement for "first walking gentleman" (a term given to the line of characters played) at the Theatre Royal, Edinburgh, and opened on the 9th inst.

You will naturally ask me how I like the change. Briefly then— very much. The study is incessant, but at the theatre you are surrounded by cheerful and happy faces, who greet you with a smile and a merry word, and at home your mind is occupied by new parts. There is no formal restraint, no petty subjection of one to another—because they are equals—they work for a prize free to all.

As a body, actors are an independent, intellectual, good-natured, very polite, and eccentric class of beings. The ladies are generally superior to the average standard of their sex. The Theatre is a very comfortable, systematic place; fines are imposed for misconduct and neglect, and no smoking or drinking is allowed.

My Mother and Father would unite their very kind regards with, my dear Mrs Wilkins.—Yours very sincerely,

J. H. BRODRIBB.

P.S.—When you reply, please direct to—
Mr H. Irving,
Mrs Robart's,
17 Elder Street,
Edinboro'.

Excuse this disjointed scrawl.

Irving in "The Bells"

At his entrance the applause was so instantaneous that it became part of the play. . . . It was no boisterous greeting by an excitable race, for a blustering actor—it was something which can only be described as part and parcel of the whole, as right as rain. It was a torrent while it lasted. Power responded to power. This applause was no false note, whereas silence would have been utterly false; for though Irving endured and did not accept the applause, he deliberately called it out of the spectators. It was necessary *to them*—not to him; it was something they had to experience, or to be rid of, or rather released from, before they could exactly take in what he was going to give them.

So then the applause came down like thunder as Irving appeared in the doorway with the ordinary cry: "It is I." Now no one has ever been known to hear these words distinctly—they resolved themselves into a single exclamation. The door flung open—the figure is in the room, God knows how—with arms extended, face alight, and this single ejaculation: " 't'sI." . . .

The process of getting rid of his coat, and brushing off the snow as he stands on the mat by the door being over, he works his way down to a chair in the centre (Irving was always in the centre—he had no inferiority complex), and there, taking off his boots, he begins to put on and buckle his shoes. Now you might think that the act of taking off some boots could be done in one way only—but the way Irving did it had never been thought of till he did it, and has never been done since. It was, in every gesture, every half move, in the play of his shoulders, legs, head, and arms, mesmeric in the highest degree— slowly we were drawn to watch every inch of his work as we are drawn to read and linger on every syllable of a strangely fine writer.

It was the perfection of craftsmanship.

from *Henry Irving* by E. G. Craig

The Crystal Palace

The Queen's Exhibition Journal 1851

May 1   This day is one of the greatest and most glorious days of our lives, with which, to my pride and joy, the name of my dearly beloved Albert is for ever associated. It is a day which makes my heart swell with thankfulness. . . .

The Park presented a wonderful spectacle, crowds streaming through it,—carriages and troops passing, quite like the Coronation, and for *me*, the same anxiety. The day was bright and all bustle and excitement. At ½ p. 11 the whole procession in 9 State carriages was set in motion. Vicky and Bertie were in our carriage (the other children and Vivi did not go). Vicky was dressed in lace over white satin, with a small wreath of pink wild roses in her hair, and looked very nice. Bertie was in full Highland dress. The Green Park and Hyde Park were one mass of densely crowded human beings, in the highest good humour and most enthusiastic. I never saw Hyde Park look as it did, being filled with crowds as far as the eye could reach. A little rain fell, just as we started, but before we neared the Crystal Palace, the sun shone and gleamed upon the gigantic edifice, upon which the flags of every nation were flying. We drove up Rotten Row and got out of our carriages at the entrance on that side. The glimpse, through the iron gates of the Transept, the waving palms and flowers, the myriads of people filling the galleries and seats around, together with the flourish of trumpets as we entered the building, gave a sensation I shall never forget, and I felt much moved. . . .

The sight as we came to the centre where the steps and chair (on which I did *not* sit) was placed, facing the beautiful crystal fountain was magic and impressive. The tremendous cheering, the joy expressed in every face, the vastness of the building, with all its decorations and exhibits, the sound of the organ (with 200 instruments and 600 voices, which seemed nothing) and my beloved husband, the creator of this peace festival "uniting the industry and art of all nations of the earth", all this was indeed moving, and a day to live for ever. God bless my dearest Albert, and my dear Country, which has shown itself so great to-day.

All the Commissioners and the Executive Committee etc. who had worked so hard and to whom such immense praise is due, seemed truly happy, and no one more so than Paxton, who may feel justly proud. He rose from an ordinary gardener's boy! Every one was astounded and delighted. The return was equally satisfactory, the crowd most enthusiastic, and perfect order kept. We reached the Palace at 20 m. past 1 and went out on the balcony, being loudly cheered. The Pce and Pcess were quite delighted and impressed. That *we* felt happy and thankful, I need not say, proud of all that had passed and of my beloved's success. I was more impressed by the scene I had witnessed than words can say. Dearest Albert's name is for ever immortalized, and the absurd reports of dangers of every kind and sort, put out by a set of people—the "soi-disant" fashionables and the most violent protectionists,—are silenced.

May 11th, 1851

. . . I was not purposing to go near the Exhibition myself—I had not so much as gone to view the outside since it was roofed in. But the other day Forster offered us his Examiner-ticket (i.e. a press ticket for his paper *The Examiner*) which admitted both Mr C. and *a lady*—so we went and oh how tired I was! Not that it was not really a very beautiful sight—especially at the entrance; the three large trees, *built in, because the people objected to their being cut down*, a crystal fountain, and a large blue canopy give one a momentary impression of a Bazaar in the *Arabian Nights Entertainments*; and such a lot of things of different kinds and of well dressed people—for the tickets were still 5/- —was rather imposing for a few minutes; but when you come to look at the wares in detail there was nothing really worth looking at—at least that one could not have seen *samples* of in the shops. The big diamond indeed—worth a million! *that* one could not have seen at any jeweller's; but oh Babbie what a disappointment! for the big diamond—unset—looked precisely like a bit of crystal the size and shape of the first joint of your thumb! And the fatigue of even the most cursory survey was indescribable, and to tell you the God's truth I would not have given the pleasure of reading a good Fairy Tale for all the pleasure to be got from that "Fairy Scene!"

from *Letters* by Jane Welsh Carlyle

Uncle. "So, you've been to the Crystal Palace—Have you, Gus!"
Gus. "Yes, Uncle."
Uncle. "Well, now, I'll give you Sixpence if you will tell me what you admired most in that Temple of Industry!"
Gus. (unhesitatingly). "Veal and 'Am Pies, and the Ginger Beer. Give us the Sixpence!"

The Seaside

The Seaside
In and Out of The Season

In summer-time it was a paradise
Of mountain, frith, and bay, and shining sand;
Our outward rowers sang towards the land,
Follow'd by waving hands and happy cries:
By the full flood the groups no longer roam;
And when, at ebb, the glistening beach grows wide,
No barefoot children race into the foam,
But passive jellies wait the turn of tide.
Like some forsaken lover, lingering there,
The boatman stands; the maidens trip no more
With loosen'd locks; far from the billows' roar
The Mauds and Maries knot their tresses fair,
Where not a foam-flake from th'enamour'd shore
Comes down the sea-wind on the golden hair.

by Charles Tennyson-Turner

Brighton in "The Season"

London *plus* prawns for breakfast and the sea air. Blessings on the sea air, which gives you an appetite to eat them!

from *Punch*, October 1845

"Ramsgate Sands" by William P. Frith

Fashionable Watering Places

Thirty years ago Margate and Ramsgate were crowded in the season by those who now would not be seen but at Brighton, and perhaps will not continue to go there long. It requires marvellous courage now to confess any interest in places so utterly discarded by fashion as are Margate and Ramsgate. They are still crowded, but by decidedly unfashionable people. To those who remember the former place "in its glory" it must be strange to read the historian's account of it a hundred years ago.

"Meregate seems to have had its name from there being a gate or way into the sea, which lies just by a little *Mere* called by the inhabitants now the Brooks. It is a small fishing town, irregularly built, and the houses very low; and has formerly been of good repute for the fishing and coasting trade."

The erection of the delightful and very magnificent pier, which is indeed most deservedly the pride of Ramsgate, has doubtless mainly contributed to obtain for this agreeable, albeit now unfashionable, watering-place the high reputation it has gained.

How shall we give the picture of to-day? We cannot do it: we will offer the materials, and our readers will combine them at pleasure.

Look at these sands! They appear one indiscriminate moving mass of cabs, cars, carts, and carriages; horses, ponies, dogs, donkies, and boys; men, women, children, and nurses; and, the least and the biggest—babies and bathing-machines.

Imagine of course all proper associations and accompaniments: little boys with spades; nurses with babies; mammas with sewing; young ladies with novels; young gentlemen with Byron, canes, and eye-glasses; older ones with newspapers, sticks, and spectacles.

Then the hawkers are a most noisy, important, and persevering fraternity here: such opportunities for "cheap bargains"; nothing in the world that you mayn't buy, from a puppy-dog to "a yard of cushion-lace, real thread, for the low price of one penny farthing"; from a pincushion to a garden-chair; from a memorial of the Deluge, in the shape of a Folkstone fossil, to a sample of modern skill in the form of a threepenny doll; from a "splendid set" of ornaments of Derbyshire spar, to a nightcap, a pair of garters, or a watch-pocket.

"Confusion worse confounded," may indeed aptly characterize the scene on a bright, warm morning, "in the Season". Yet is the happy turmoil not at its height. Oh, no! A SHOWER COMES: despite the blue sky, despite the weather-glasses, the almanacs, and everything else, a sudden and most unprovoked shower comes—comes pepperingly, and without notice. Alas, then! for the gossamer bonnets—the primrose tulle, and the pink crape: alas! for the fair ones whose ringlets and whose habiliments are alike of summer-day strength: alas! for the mammas who cannot keep pace in the retreat with their fairy-footed daughters; and alas! and a double alas! for the stout and portly papas, who, unceremoniously interrupted in the middle of Peel's speech by a sudden shower-bath, look up, and ejaculate "very extraordinary!" but finding that not-withstanding this oracular demonstration of their suprise the rain continues, ay, and in earnest too, hastily turn up their collars, button their coats, thrust their spectacles into one pocket, at the same time dropping the case from the other, crush the newspaper under one arm, grasp their stick with the other hand, and set off sturdily after their wives and daughters; first, however, casting another glance at the pitiless horizon, and again ejaculating loudly, "very extraordinary!"

Meanwhile the chairs are set as for a game at leapfrog, to keep the seats dry; and the nurses, and babies, and donkies, and boys, are all huddled together under the awnings of the bathing-machines by this time drawn up in order under the cliff. . . . Just as all these arrangements are satisfactorily completed, the raindrops cease, the cloud has passed over, the sun comes out bright and brilliant, and the whole horizon is laughing in his beams. Papas and mammas have had enough of such "very extraordinary" weather; they return not, but the younger people do. The chairs resume their "native" position; the bipeds and quadrupeds emerge from the shelter of the bathing-machines, the donkies shaking their ears, and the nurse-maids their bonnets: and the sands, which three minutes before were "full of desolation", are again ringing with life and merriment.

from *Chronicles of Fashion* by Elizabeth Stone

Ladies Bathing

The ceremony of ladies bathing is accompanied with some peculiarities. Owing to the rapid rise and fall of the tide they are obliged to be particularly quick in their movements, so that not only those who are about to dip are as busy as bees, but likewise the mothers, and aunts, and sisters, and cousins, and friends, who attend them. And perhaps it is this appearance of bustle that always attracts a gang of idlers who, having nothing better to do, stand by and look on. Notwithstanding a painted board, placed in a conspicuous position in the rear of a score or upwards of bathing machines standing in a line, explicitly decrees that those of the gentlemen shall not advance nearer than one hundred yards to those of the ladies, I did not remark any specific regulations enforced as to distance among the spectators, which point seemed otherwise decided by common consent to everybody's satisfaction. However, all pleasure-boats are prohibited from approaching within the distance of thirty yards, under the penalty, in case of contempt of the regulation, of five shillings; a fine which, under the circumstances, cannot be called exorbitant. I am not aware how it is proposed to adjust a case of disputed distance, some favour being properly due to the variation of the steersman's eye on such an occasion; the fine has been calculated, probably, by those best able to assess the damage, and affords the means of turning, in these liberal days, even a lady's charms to the good of the parish. While the insulted fair one becomes a public benefactress, the gentleman fined, provided his eyes be tolerably good, has no cause to complain of the draft on his purse; the fine, moreover, falls on the boat's crew ñot exceeding, at all events, a few pence per naked lady.

All the old bathing-women at Southport are young men, that is to say, stout lusty fellows under middle age. Whether the service diminishes the chilling effects of the water; whether it makes young men old, or old men young, is a point, they say, not yet determined; at all events, such is the force of habit, that the young ladies one and all, without hesitation, submit to their guidance, such as they are. The guide, or male personage, or what not, takes his post in front of the door of the machine, in the usual manner, while the young lady within disencumbers herself of her apparel, putting on a dark blue bathing dress, in which, by the way, I perceived no other difference from those commonly used, than that it was invariably fastened with strings between the ancles. In this costume the fair one, after a few minutes' delay, reappears on the upper step of the sanctuary, and there stands timidly hesitating—Presenting both hands to the guide, supported by his grasp, and falling backwards on the wave, she then receives the embraces of old Neptune as young ladies usually do, with the accompaniments of squeaking, giggling, kicking, splashing, and wincing.

from *Home Tour* by Sir George Head

Mermaids at play

Come to Your Martha

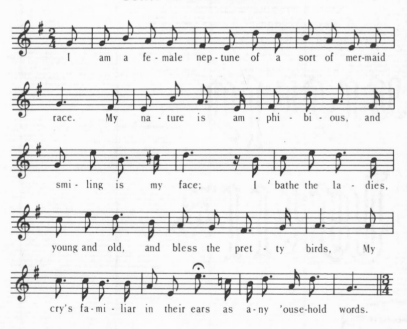

I am a fe-male nep-tune of a sort of mer-maid race. My na-ture is am-phi-bi-ous, and smi-ling is my face; I 'bathe the la - dies, young and old, and bless the pret - ty birds, My cry's fa-mi - liar in their ears as a-ny 'ouse-hold words.

SPOKEN: *Good morning Mum, and how are you and the young ladies?*
Glad to see you down again, and the young gentlemen agrowing fine men,
as don't forget the time when their old Martha carried 'em a kicking
and a screaming into the water. Bless their pretty limbs! No mum if you
ask me—seven is not too many for one bathing machine in the season—
step up my dears and don't fall out the other side Chorus

Come to your Mar - tha, come, come, come, The
wa - ter is warm in the sun, sun, sun; Don't
shi - ver dear, there's nought to fear, But
come to your Mar - tha come.

I has to study customers, and if the sea is rough,
My manner is so smooth, I make 'em think it calm enough;
Though timid ones when they behold the ocean cold and grey,
If I was not to collar 'em, would quickly run away.

SPOKEN: *The bathing machine door is like a dentist's, when you get*
there you want to turn back. It was only yesterday a lady says, "Do
you think it safe? my children are so delicate." "Safe Mum," I says,
"Griffith's safes isn't in it. Ain't I a mother with fourteen, and three
lots of twins, and a husband, when not in liquor, a boat-builder, and
earning good money?" "Are you sure these towels are well aired?"
"Aired Mum," I says. "They've been a airing ever since you was down
last year." "But I fear the sea is very cold." "Cold!" I says, "Bless the
lady, ain't I just been and poured a kettle of boiling water in it?"
Chorus

There's not in the Aquarium, or yet within the sea,
Such pretty little fishes as come down to bathe with me;
You will not see a fairer sight in this or any town,
Than twenty hanging on to ropes, and bobbing up and down.

SPOKEN: *"Isn't the water jolly this morning Julia? Don't splash me Kate or I'll tell Ma. See me swim, I get on very well till I take my feet off the ground, then I get a mouth full of salt water. Martha, there's a man with a telescope." "Like his brazen imperence my dear." "Here's a wave coming Martha! Martha!"* Chorus

I ain't alone the favourite of Ma's and the pretty girls,
I've bathed a many markisses and dipped a many a earls;
They were but young, but if they could remember it they'd say
With you, that Martha Gunn is quite a great *gun* in her way.

SPOKEN: *"We're all equals when we're in the water,"* as the poet says, *"Am I not a woman and a bather."* There's a good saying, *"Go to Bath,"* certainly, and the oftener the better. Bathing strengthens the interlect, braces the body, clears the system, puts new life in the blood, old heads on young shoulders, fills the pocket, drives away care, cures corns, warts, bunions, Pilgrims progresses, water on the brain, new-ralgia, old ralgia, velocipedes, bicycles, telephones, tella-creams, and all the Primrose 'ills as flesh is heir to, so* Chorus

Bathing Places

One more word upon the almost heathen indecency of our bathing-places, which makes one think that much of our boasted refinement is but surface deep. In most places but Britain, male bathers are compelled to wear some sort of decent covering, such as short drawers, which do not in the least impede the movements of the body; it should be imperative in this country also, and one might give a hint that the present indecency is not diminished by the unblushing intrusiveness of some of the fair sex.

from *Health Resorts of Great Britain* by Dr Spencer Thomson

Seaside scene by "Phiz"

To Thomas Carlyle,
  Scotsbrig

Pier Hotel, Ryde.
Wednesday morning, August 9th, 1843.

We reached Ryde at eight in the evening, and, the second hotel being filled, had to take up our quarters for that night at the first, which "is the dearest hotel in Europe", and the hotel in Europe, so far as I have seen, where there is the least human comfort. I had to make tea from an urn the water of which was certainly not "as hot as one could drink it"; the cream was blue milk, the butter tasted of straw, and the "cold fowl" was a *lukewarm* one, and as tough as leather. After this insalubrious repast finding that, beyond sounding the depths of vacuum, there was nothing to be done that night, I retired to my bed. The windows looked over house-roofs and the sea, so I hoped it would be quiet; but, alas, there was a dog uttering a volley of loud barks, about once in the five minutes, and rousing up what seemed to be a whole infinitude of dogs in the distance! Of course, fevered and nervous as I was at any rate from the journey, I could not sleep at all;

I do not mean that *I slept ill*, but I have absolutely *never been asleep at all the whole night*! So you may fancy the favourable mood I am in towards Ryde this morning! I feel as if I would not pass another night in that bed for a hundred pounds!

Nor shall I need. Clark has been out this morning to seek a lodging; and has found one, he says, very quiet, quite away from the town. If I cannot sleep *there*, I will return to my own red bed as fast as possible.

from Letters by Jane Welsh Carlyle

Punch and Judy show

Sport

Derby Day

Racing at Epsom. Today is Derby day, a gala occasion. Parliament relaxes: for three days nothing but horses and their trainers has been talked of.

The Derby is a large, green plain, slightly undulating; to one side are three grandstands for the public, and several smaller stands. Facing these are tents and hundreds of booths, stables improvised under canvas, and an incredible muddle of carts and carriages and coaches, horses, horsemen and private omnibuses. There are perhaps two hundred thousand people here.

For it is, indeed, a fair: the people have come to enjoy themselves uproariously. There are gypsies everywhere, singers and dancers grotesquely got up as negroes; booths for shooting with bow and carbine, cheap-jacks selling watch-chains with a torrent of eloquence, games of skittles, and Aunt Sally, all kinds of musicians, and the most astonishing procession of cabs, coaches, droskis, four-in-hands, each with its baskets of pies and pastries, cold meats, melon, fruit and wine, especially champagne. They are being unpacked; everyone is going to eat and drink, it will restore and raise their animal spirits; noisy, full-blooded enjoyment and loud, candid laughter are products of a full stomach.

A bell began ringing: the race was about to begin. Three or four hundred policemen clear the course; the stands are crammed with spectators and the fields facing them are one great dark stain of heads. We go up to our seats: nothing of grandeur to be seen. At this distance crowds become insect swarms; horsemen and carriages passing and recrossing each other look like beetles and cockchafers, or great bumble-bees crawling over a green carpet. The jockeys in their red, blue, yellow or mauve stand out apart, like a group of butterflies alighted. No doubt I am lacking in enthusiasm, but I find it like watching a game played by insects.

Thirty-four starters: after three false starts they are off. Fifteen or

"Derby Day" by William P. Frith

twenty keep together in a mass, the rest are in small groups as you see them coming up the course. To the eye the speed does not look very great: like that of a train seen from a couple of miles away, when the coaches look like toys being pulled along by a child. Here, certainly, the physical impression is no more impressive, and such words as "hurricane" would be very out of place.

For several minutes, then, the brown mark dotted with red and other colours, moves steadily along against the distant green background. It turns a corner and the first group is coming our way. "Hat's off!"—all heads are uncovered and the crowd surges to its feet. A throttled cheer breaks out in the grandstands. Cold faces are now lit up with warmth, phlegmatic bodies twitch and jerk and gesticulate; below, in the betting rings, the shock of movement is extraordinary, like a sudden universal St Vitus' dance. Imagine a crowd of automata receiving an electric shock and gesticulating with all their limbs like mad semaphores. But the most curious spectacle is the human tide which immediately and suddenly breaks and spreads over the course behind the horses, like a flood of ink: the still, dark mass has melted and flowed; in an instant it spreads wide and vast, as far as one can see; now it is in front of the stands. Three or four lines of policemen form a living fence, and when necessary use their fists to keep a clear space where the horses and their jockeys arrive for weighing out and checking. There is one big moment in the race, when the horses are only two hundred paces away: in an instant the speed becomes suddenly apparent and the group of riders and mounts flashes ahead, and words like "tempest" are no longer out of place.

An unknown horse, Caractacus, has won, by a short head. The odds against him were forty to one, whereas others, very famous horses, started at three to one, two to one, nine to two: a *débacle* for betting men. The prize, with accessories, amounts to £6,775; counting his bets the owner will win about a milllion francs. We hear of enormous losses, £20,000, £50,000: last year a colonel shot himself after the big race, for he realized that he was ruined; had he awaited the outcome of the other races he would have won enough to pay his debts. Just as the race was starting, the owner of one of the private stands had shouted that he would lay all his takings on Buckstone. Several cabbies lost their horses and cabs, having gambled them away.

We make our way down from the stand: the stairs and buffets are crammed to the point of suffocation; but most carriage and omnibus parties have brought their own food and the people settle down to feast in the open, in small groups. Good humour and gladness abound. The classes mingle.

Meanwhile, all over the plain, jaws were working, bottles being emptied and, towards evening, the fun of the fair was at its height. Twenty-four gentlemen triumphantly set up seventy-five bottles on their omnibus—they had drunk them all. Parties bombarded each other with chicken-bones, lobster shells and divots of turf. Two parties of gentlemen had got down from their omnibus and were boxing ten against ten; one had two teeth broken. There were some grotesque incidents: three men and a lady were standing on top of their carriage, the horse made a movement and all four fell off, the lady with her legs in the air: roars of laughter. Little by little the fumes of wine were going to their heads: these people, so coldly correct in their manners, so delicate in their behaviour, began behaving very oddly. Several gentlemen went up to a carriage containing ladies and young girls, and there, against the wheel eased themselves: the mother tried to drive them off with her umbrella.

On the way back the road disappeared beneath clouds of dust. Parts of the downs had been worn quite bare by feet. We were all horribly dirty and white with dust. There were drunks in the road the whole way back; at eight that night they were still to be seen at Hyde Park Corner, reeling about and being sick. Their laughing cronies supported them and the faces of spectators did not express any disgust. Nothing is barred to-day; it is an outlet for a whole year's constraint.

from Notes on England, 1860–70 by Hippolyte Taine

Blood Sports

About ten years ago there was a cock-fight in Birmingham, but the police interrupted it, and apprehended about 100 persons. They were all brought before the magistrates and bound over not to offend again either as spectators or principals. So long as fox-hunting, coursing and horse-racing are allowed by law, I do not see why cock-fighting should be forbidden.

from Amusements of the People

The English country gentleman galloping after a fox—the unspeakable in full pursuit of the uneatable (*Oscar Wilde*)

A Plot Exposed

The mains at Chester and Preston, where Viscount Molyneux, Mr Henry Bold Houghton, Lord Derby, and that king of cockers, old Doctor Bellyse, of Audlem, fought their priceless duck-wings and black-breasted reds, were famous throughout England, not only for the excellence of the birds, but for the amount of the stakes, as much as £50,000 sometimes depending on a match.

Well, these gentlemen of Failsworth were enthusiastic cockers . . . and the cocking match between "the Gentlemen of Failsworth" and "the Gentlemen of Manchester" caused considerable interest. . . .

On the first day thirteen very hard battles were fought, and at the close Failsworth was three ahead. Booth, the well-known feeder, fed for Failsworth, and Hankinson, of Pendleton, for Manchester. On the evening as the Failsworth gentlemen were enjoying their after-dinner cigars in the bar-parlour of the Three Tuns, the harmony of the proceedings was interrupted by a furious row at the bar. On inquiring, the originators of the rumpus turned out to be one of the Manchester party—a lame gentleman, named Churchill—and Booth, the Failsworth feeder. The former had accused the latter of having played him false, and, both being in their cups, the whole villainy came out.

Mr Churchill, it appeared, had paid Booth handsomely to "queer" the Failsworth cocks; but the professional had pocketed the money, and, after all, acted on the square. Booth admitted having done this, and his excuse was that he had taken the money in order to make matters even between himself and Mr Churchill in respect to an old unsettled score, but that he had never meant to act otherwise than fairly by his own party, and throw the tempters over. Of course, there was a tremendous noise after these extraordinary disclosures, and when the parties met the next morning at the Pit, the Failsworth gentlemen declined to go on with the match, on the ground that their opponents had been distinctly convicted of foul play.

from *Famous Fights—Past and Present* edited by Harold Furniss

The Wedgefield Wake

At Wedgefield at one village Wake,
The cockers all did meet,
At Billy Lane's the cockfighters,
To have a special treat.

For Charley Mason's spangles cock
Was matched to fight a red
That came from Wil'n'all o'er the field,
And belonged to Cheeky Ned.

Ri-too-ler-oo la-roo-la-roo ri-too-la-roo-la-ray
With a clicking and a clacking and a clucking all day,
Ho ho a clip winged red and a spangled grey.

The finer birds in any pit
There never yet were sin,
Though the Wedgefield men declared
Their cock was sure to win.

The cocks fought well and feathers flew
All round about the pit,
While blood from both of them did flow,
Yet neither would submit.

At last the spangled Wedgefield bird
Began to show defeat,
When Billy Lane he up and swore
The cock should not be beat.

For he would fight the biggest man
That came from Wil'n'all town,
Then on the word old cheeky Ned
Got up and knocked him down.

To fight they went like two bulldogs,
As it is now well known,
Till cheeky Ned seized big Bill's thumb
And bit it into the bone.

At this the Wedgefield men began
Their comrade's part to take,
And never was a fiercer fight
Fought at a village wake.

They beat the men from Wil'n'all
Back to their town again,
And long they will remember
This Wedgefield Wake and Main.

Anon.

Bull- and Badger-Baiting in Birmingham

Badger-baiting was almost as common as cock-fighting, and was carried on principally in an open space of ground in Smallbrook-street, on which a church is now being erected. A hole was dug in the ground, in which the badger was placed. There were generally a good many dogs ready to attack it in the hole, and one by one they were allowed to try to dislodge the badger, the owner of each dog paying a stipulated sum for the privilege of running his dog at the animal. Bull-baiting was a more costly, and consequently a rarer source of amusement. One bull was often baited on three or four successive Mondays. There was generally a baiting match at the three great "wakes" or local fairs, held annually at Birmingham. Chapel wake was the best of sports of all kinds, and an unusual amount of bull-baiting, cock-fighting, badger-baiting, dancing, singing and sight-seeing was there indulged in.

from Amusements of the People

Tom Sayers, Champion of England

You lovers of the pugilistic ring, attend with mirth and cheers,
Whilst I here pen down and will expound the merits of Tom Sayers,
He is the noble champion, who in honour does uphold
The belt of merry England, and her laurels tipp'd with gold.

His first battle was with Andy Crouch in the year '49,
He polished off that hardy son, in 13 minutes time;
He fought next with Dan Collins, and in round then full two
    score,
He thrashed his brave opponent in minutes 84.

He fought the Tipton Slasher, and brought him to the dust,
And on the banks of Medway he emptied many a purse;
He conquered the great Bill Bainge, and Tom Paddock of Redditch,
So brave a man as Tommy Sayers ne'er came from proud Sussex.

And last he fought Bob Brettle, a man of courage bold,
Whose mighty deeds of manly art the pages does unfold;
But from an accidental fall, Bob Brettle he must yield,
Leaving Tom Sayers the winner, and the victor of the field.

Now the praises of Tom Sayers, I could not full extol,
He's the champion of proud England, and the conquerer of all;
His manly determination, as in the ring he does appear,
Declares him as the Champion, the Belt of England to wear.

Anon.

The Fight for the Championship
(between Tom Sayers and John Carmel Heenan)

Umpires and a referee having now been appointed, the signal was given to prepare for the combat. The first ceremony, that of tying the colours to the stakes, was then proceeded with, and no time was cut to waste in doffing their upper toggery. Heenan was the first to appear in buff, and a single glance was sufficient to show that his condition was all that could be required by the most fastidious. Tom's mahogany bust was quickly after bared to the gaze of the multitude, and here, too, was evidence of strict attention to his work. They had a final rub from their seconds, and now advanced to give the final friendly shake. This was the time to get a fair idea of their respective proportions, and in size it really looked a horse to a hen. Heenan stood full $4\frac{1}{2}$ inches over Tom, and had an immense advantage in length. Every muscle on his broad back, his shoulders, and arms, was well developed, and gave evidence of enormous power. His legs are rather light, but still there is no lack here of wire and activity. His skin was exceedingly fair and transparent, and shone like that of a thorough-bred. His mug was hard, and looked older than we expected, his cheek-bones being very prominent, and now that they had been denuded of much that was superfluous, his *tout ensemble* was far more like that of his brother professional than in his first interview with us. Tom looked brown and hard as nails: his well-knit frame seemed fitter than we have seen it for years. He looked visibly older even than when he fought Brettle, but considering what he has gone through, this is not to be wondered at. The only points in which there appeared any advantage on his side were in his loins and his legs, which were cast in a decidedly stronger mould than those of his towering opponent.

The Fight

Round 1. Heenan at once threw himself into very fair position, his left well balanced ready for a shoot, and the right across the body. Tom's position was the same as ever, lightly but firmly planted on his pins. He smiled and nodded, and on Heenan trying to lead off his left, got well back.

3. After a little lively fiddling, Tom got too near to the big-un, who

instantly slung out his left straight and full on the bridge of Tom's beak, knocking him clean off his pins. [*First knock down* for Heenan.]

6. Tom's countenance, though not swelled, still was much flushed, while the Boy was almost scatheless. He was somewhat wild, and tried both hands, but missed. Counter-hits ensued, in which Tom received the full weight of Heenan's ponderous fist on his right arm, which was driven back against his face. Tom reached Heenan's left cheek, leaving his mark. Heenan retaliated on the right brow, and Tom fell.

7. Tom's right peeper displayed marks of pepper, and it was perceptible that he had sustained severe injury to his right arm, which was beginning to swell, and which he now kept close to his body, as if to support it. Still he went to Heenan in his corner, and that hero delivered his left, but not effectively on the chest. Tom danced away, and as he turned round napped a little one from the right on his back.

This round lasted 13 minutes, and was a fine specimen of stratagem and skill, especially on the part of Tom. His right arm now was much swollen, and so painful, that he could make little or no use of it.

8. Tom slowest to the call of time, but directly he was at the scratch the Boy retired to his corner, whither Tom had to follow him. Heenan at once let go his left, but Tom laughed and jumped back. A slight exchange followed, and Tom napped a straight one on the sniffer. Heenan now missed a couple of well-meant shots, and Tom jumped away from a third, and as he turned his back upon Heenan got a right-hander on the back of the neck.

36. The Benicia Boy's face was a spectacle to behold, while Tom was very weak. The Boy rushed to a close, and caught Tom round the neck, dragging him to the ropes. At this time the police, who had been gradually making their way to the ring, began a violent struggle to get close and put a stop to hostilities. The Boy tried to hold Tom, but the latter slipped through his arms and fell.

37 and last. Tom was first up, and seemed the better man; he made his left twice on Heenan's eye, and the latter at length caught him round the neck at the ropes and there held him. Tom's efforts to extricate himself were vain, but he administered severe punishment to the Boy's face. The police at this time got closer, there was a rush to the ropes from all sides, and we, in company with others, including the referee, were completely shut out from the view. We are informed

that the round ended in both going to grass at the expiration of *two hours and six minutes.*

Heenan's face (after the fight)

The English Cup Final

The Oval on Saturday was a sight. Londoners themselves were amazed at the host of people that rose up on all sides of the field of play, a solid bank of humanity. . . . The kick-off was punctuality itself, and when the ball was set moving by Hunter, the Albion had an immediate advantage in a steady breeze that blew from goal to goal, and they also had the fall of the ground in their favour. A few long interchanges took place, and then the Albion bore down on the Villa goal. Without entering into the minutiae, it may be said that in the first half the meteorological advantages were fully taken advantage of by the Albion. . . . But, having all the best of the play, the Albion failed to score.

When ends were changed, their chance of victory had to all appearances fled. Had the wretched state of the ground not told so severely against the short passing game of the Villa forwards, there is no saying how many goals they would have piled up. Again and again they worked the ball down, when it would stick in the soft mire, ere it reached the man it was passed to, or a delicate screw would be spoiled by an exasperating slip. . . . At length Hunter made a judicious pass to Davis, when everyone thought he would rush for goal himself; Davis ran down and shot from the wing; the ball was well gauged, and as it dropped just beyond Roberts, Hodgetts took a step forward, and catching it on the side of the foot, it went through the goal. It looked surprisingly like off-side of Hodgetts, but the officials dismissed the appeals. . . . A minute before time, when hard pressed, Horton kicked the ball softly into goal for Roberts to get it. Hunter saw the dodge, down he pounced on Roberts, both came to the ground, and stretching out his leg the Villa captain, with a mighty effort, made the second goal for his side, and the game was won by 2 goals to 0.

Reception of the News in Birmingham

The reception of the welcome news in Birmingham sent the Villa supporters wild with joy, and excited the liveliest satisfaction in all football circles throughout the town. The various resorts which the leather chasing fraternity are in the habit of frequenting were during the afternoon besieged by large crowds anxious to receive the earliest reports of the progress of the game. . . . The practice which certain well known Villa patrons have for a long time followed of competing with the evening papers by displaying private telegrams in the windows giving the results of important matches was developed on Saturday afternoon to a remarkable extent. At one or two of these places private messages were received nearly every quarter of an hour. . . . The most remarkable scenes took place in the Lozells and Aston New Town. Here football tobacconists and publicans are very thick on the ground, and in every window the progress and result of the struggle was promptly chronicled. One non-football observer, who passed through the district shortly after 6 o'clock, gave it as his serious opinion that the Lozells had gone mad. To an uninformed, and therefore unsympathizing mind, there was certainly much in the appearance of the street to warrant a strong suspicion that the neighbourhood had gone off its head. From William Street to the Six Ways the road was thronged by a crowd which must have numbered several thousands. . . .

from *The Birmingham Daily Mail*, Monday April 4th 1887

Aston Villa team, 1886–87

The National Cup

The winter game appears to have its commercial as well as its re-creative side. One Black Country town has suddenly awakened to the fact that its shopkeepers are being materially injured, because on a Saturday afternoon thousands of its working men are attracted to West Bromwich to see the football matches there. The wives meet the husbands after the game is over, or sometimes husband and wife both patronize the sport, and the result is that the Saturday's shopping, or most of it, is done at West Bromwich, and not in their own town. Things have come to such a pass that Oldbury has started a club in self-defence, and the leading tradesmen are finding the sinews of war. This is the latest development of the football mania, and perhaps other popular centres that are not already supplied with a football club will be hastening in their own interest to supply the want, as a very necessary means of combining business with pleasure. The advance that football has made in public favour, more particularly among the working classes, during the last few years, is simply marvellous. Ten years ago it would have been impossible to create one half of the excitement in the town and suburbs and throughout the Black Country, even though a Birmingham club had won the cup twice over. There is certainly no other sport upon which such an intense feeling of harmless partisanship could centre, or which could induce thousands of people to wait in the streets for the result, as though the fate of the Empire was trembling in the balance. Football in itself is a manly game, bringing into play all the best qualities of the muscular athlete, and anything that gives the hard-worked artisan wholesome out-door amusement is entitled to every encouragement. And now that the great winter pastime commends itself as a factor in the revival of trade to the commercial community, who can say what fresh developments are not in store for it?

from *The Birmingham Daily Mail*, Monday April 4th 1887

The Deserted Parks

"Solitudinem faciunt: Parcum appelant"

Amidst thy bowers the tyrant's hand is seen,
The rude pavilions sadden all thy green;
One selfish pastime grasps the whole domain,
And half a faction swallows up the plain;
Adown thy glades, all sacrificed to cricket,
The hollow-sounding bat now guards the wicket;
Sunk are thy mounds in shapeless level all,
Lest aught impede the swiftly rolling ball;
And trembling, shrinking from the fatal blow,
Far, far away thy hapless children go.

The man of wealth and pride
Takes up a space that many poor supplied;
Space for the game, and all its instruments,
Space for pavilions and for scorers' tents;
The ball, that raps his shins in padding cased,
Has wore the verdure to an arid waste;
His Parks, where these exclusive sports are seen,
Indignant spurns the rustic from the green;
While through the plain, consigned to silence all,
In barren splendour flits the russet ball.

by Lewis Carroll

The Famous United XI

The rival of the All England Eleven, the United Eleven, was composed
of principal players of the South of England with a few from the
North, notably Carpenter and one of my own countrymen, James
Grundy. No cricketer was better known in those days than Old
Jemmy. He was one of the best medium pace round-arm bowlers
then about, having great command over the ball, but had not much
break and consequently on a good wicket was not difficult; but if the
pitch broke up a little and he found a "spot", he was then very danger-

ous. This happened on one occasion when Notts and Yorkshire played on Trent Bridge. The victory appeared to be as good as won by the latter, who had few runs to get and plenty of wickets in hand. Grundy, however, got on a worn place, and kept pegging away at it with such persistency that the Yorkshiremen's wickets fell one after the other in a most remarkable manner, and the home county achieved a brilliant victory.

I never in my life, I think, saw so much excitement as was evinced by the spectators on this occasion. When the match was won the uproar was indescribable. Old Charles Brown, seeing as he thought inevitable defeat for his county, had gone home and to bed hours before, and many of the spectators, surrounding his house on their way from the ground, made Charlie get up and put his head out of the window to hear the result of the match, which he no sooner understood than he declared he would dress himself and come out and make a night of it, which I have no doubt he did.

Grundy always wore a black velvet cap, which, when bowling, he generally took off and thrust in his belt. His delivery was wonderfully easy, and he could bowl for almost any length of time without fatigue. He was a remarkably neat, bright-looking man, always as keen as possible when in the field. He had a great weakness for fat mutton chops and would devour it all eagerly. He once at Lord's bowled to George Parr and myself twenty-one overs without our scoring a run.

Tom Hearne was another most useful all-round man. He made lots of runs and took plenty of wickets. He was more successful with the old-fashioned "draw" than any batsman I can remember. In a match at Islington a curious incident occurred. A pigeon came flying across the ground high in the air, at which Hearne threw the ball, hit the bird, which dropped dead at his feet. The pigeon Tom afterwards had stuffed.

Of William Caffyn's play I cannot speak too highly. It is a pity such players as he should ever grow old. A superior man in every way was Caffyn. He always dressed well, and had a smart and neat appearance at all times. I have often heard related a trick which that great practical joker, Sam Parr, once played him during a tour they were on. Caffyn always took with him when travelling a hat-box, in which was a splendid tall silk hat that he wore on Sundays.

W. G. Grace, a famous Victorian cricketer

Well, during this tour Sam Parr happened to find a dead mouse, which, having flattened out as well as he could, he deposited under the lining of Caffyn's hat. This was early in the week, and the weather being very hot the head vermin soon began to be very offensive. Caffyn, who kept the hat in his bedroom at the hotel where he was staying, soon perceived this, and declared something was wrong with the drains; but when Sunday came, and the hat was required, of course the mystery was solved. He at once suspected who had played him the trick, and was so exasperated that Sam thought it advisable to keep out of his way for some time after.

John Wisden was for years one of the best all-round men in England, being a splendid fast bowler with a beautiful length, a grand little batsman, and an excellent fellow withal. Wisden was known as the "pendulum" player, from the way in which he swung his bat backwards and forwards.

As I remarked before, the match, All England Eleven v. United Eleven, was always one of the best of the season. This match was not confined to Lord's, but sometimes took place at the Oval and

85

elsewhere. Once, when it was played at Manchester, I made 111 for All England Eleven. For really enjoyable games, both for players and spectators alike, there never have been, in my opinion, and never again will be, any to equal those played between the All England Eleven and United Eleven in their best days.

from *Kings of Cricket* by Richard Daft

Vitaï Lampada

There's a breathless hush in the Close tonight—
Ten to make and the match to win—
A bumping pitch and a blinding light,
An hour to play and the last man in.
And it's not for the sake of a ribboned coat,
Or the selfish hope of a season's fame,
But his Captain's hand on his shoulder smote—
    "Play up! play up! and play the game!"

The sand of the desert is sodden red—
Red with the wreck of a square that broke;
The Gatling's jammed and the Colonel dead,
And the Regiment blind with dust and smoke,
The river of death has brimmed his banks,
And England's far and Honour a name,
But the voice of a schoolboy rallies the ranks:
    "Play up! play up! and play the game!"

This is the word that year by year,
While in her place the School is set,
Every one of her sons must hear,
And none that hears it dare forget.
This they all with a joyful mind
Bear through life like a torch in flame
And falling fling to the host behind—
    "Play up! play up! and play the game!"

by Sir Henry Newbolt

Postscript

Queen Victoria's Diamond Jubilee, 1897

THE DAILY GRAPHIC, WEDNESDAY, JANUARY 23, 1901.

DEATH OF THE QUEEN.

A PEACEFUL END.

SURROUNDED BY CHILDREN
AND GRANDCHILDREN.

MESSAGE FROM THE KING.

THE MOURNING EMPIRE.

PARLIAMENT TO MEET TO-DAY.

TRIBUTES FROM ABROAD.

Further Source Material

General Background Books

K. CHESNEY   *The Victorian Underworld*   Penguin
J. W. DODDS   *The Age of Paradox*   Gollancz
E. HALEVY   *A History of the English People in the 19th Century*   Benn
J. LAVER   *The Age of Optimism*   Weidenfeld and Nicolson
S. MARGETSON   *Leisure and Pleasure in the 19th Century*   Cassell
R. G. G. PRICE   *A History of "Punch"*   Collins
M. VICINUS   *The Industrial Muse*   Croom Helm

Contemporary Material, Autobiography, etc.

M. V. HUGHES   *A London Child of the Seventies*   O.U.P.
J. BURNETT (ed.)   *Useful Toil*   Allen Lane
H. MAYHEW   *London Labour and the London Poor*   Dover Publications
ROY PALMER (ed.)   *A Touch on the Times*   Penguin
ROY PALMER AND JON RAVEN   *The Rigs of the Fair*.   C.U.P.
E. R. PIKE   *Human Documents of the Victorian Golden Age (1850–75)*
   Allen & Unwin
V. DE SOLA PINTO AND A. E. RODWAY   *The Common Muse*   Penguin
G. A. SALA   *Twice Round the Clock*   Leicester University Press

Entertainments and Recreations

R. MANDER AND J. MITCHENSON   *Pantomime—a Story in Pictures*   Peter
   Davies
R. PEARSALL   *Victorian Popular Music*   David & Charles

Audio-visual Materials

The Victorian Era—correlated set of two colour filmstrips and one L.P.
   record (Educational Audio Visual, Coal Road, Seacroft, Leeds LS14
   2AW)
Life in Victorian England—four sets of slide folios each of 12 slides with
   recorded commentary (The Slide Centre, Portman House, 17 Broderick
   Road, London SW17 7DZ)
Parlour Song Book   Charisma, CAS 1078
A Victorian Musical Evening   Pearl, SHE 501
Mechanical Music Hall   Saydisc, SDL 232
Music Hall Top of the Bill   World Records, SHB 22   (A double album,
   every track recorded before the First World War)
Keep Your Fett Still, Geordie Hinnie   Trailer, LER 2020   (A live record-
   ing of a Tyneside Music Hall, made in 1970 but richly conveying the
   feel of the Victorian Free-and-Easy or low class Music Hall.)